EARLY
AMERICAN
METHODISM

Religion in North America

Catherine L. Albanese and Stephen J. Stein, editors

EARLY AMERICAN METHODISM

Russell E. Richey

INDIANA UNIVERSITY PRESS
Bloomington and Indianapolis

Grateful acknowledgment is made to *Methodist History* for permission to use, in revised form, the articles on which chapters 2, 4, and 6 are based.

The paper used in this publication meets the minimum requirements of American National Standard for Information Sciences—Permanence of Paper for Printed Library Materials, ANSI Z39.48-1984.

Manufactured in the United States of America

Library of Congress Cataloging-in-Publication Data

Richey, Russell E.
    Early American Methodism / Russell E. Richey
       p. cm.—(Religion in North America)
    Includes bibliographical references and index.
    ISBN 0-253-35006-9 (alk. paper)
       1. Methodist Church—United States—History—18th century.
    2. Methodist Church—United States—History—19th century.
    I. Title. II. Series.
    BX8236.R53   1991
    287′.0973′09033—dc20   91-4373

1 2 3 4 5   95 94 93 92 91

Contents

Foreword

In this volume Russell E. Richey brings a fresh perspective to the study of
a conventional Protestant denomination by highlighting the *religious*
character of early American Methodism. His essays move beyond the limits of institutional history by suggesting a new and different approach to
the examination of denominations. Richey links an anthropological sensitivity with an interest in the diverse rhetorics within Methodism between
1770 and 1810. He identifies four "languages" with which the early Methodists were conversant: a general pietistic or evangelical language, a specifically Wesleyan one, an episcopal language (after 1784), and—also
late—an American political discourse shaped during the revolutionary
and post-revolutionary years. Throughout, Richey focuses his effort to
explain early Methodism in America upon its evangelical language,
though he also explores the tensions among the various languages. Sometimes, he points out, the many tongues within Methodism have created
confusion in subsequent periods and contributed to the failure of Methodists to understand themselves. The results of Richey's vernacular choice
are instructive and impressive.

Richey is at ease, from a scholarly point of view, with the primary documents of early Methodism. He draws freely, for example, upon the journals of Jesse Lee, Freeborn Garrettson, Thomas Coke, and many others
who wrote of their life experiences. From these accounts he extracts details that limn the contours of the Methodist world, and he fills that world
with the faithful, the converts, and the inquirers. Richey is equally at ease
with the official records of the Methodists, whether minutes kept by conferences or early publications such as *The Methodist Magazine*. Out of
these he extracts far more than the usual story of institutional growth and
ecclesiastical history. Likewise, Richey is thoroughly familiar with the
scholarship on early Methodism, and he consciously crafts his essays as a
response to a number of prevailing interpretations. He ranges freely
among all of these sources, constructing a compelling argument for the
centrality of the evangelical religious experience among Methodists.

Richey carries us inside early Methodist quarterly meetings, love feasts,
conferences, and camp meetings, for it was within these structured situa-

tions that an experiential spirituality was cultivated and flourished. Moreover, Richey translates the language of that piety, giving us a sense of its substance and nuance. In his examination of the language of "fraternity," as a case in point, he demonstrates that ecclesiology and spirituality blended in the lives of itinerant circuit riders, creating something quite distinctive. The bonding among Methodist ministers underscores the link between conversion—central for every evangelical—and daily activities among the "traveling brotherhood." Not since Rhys Isaac's study of colonial Virginia have we encountered so thick and rich an account of organized religious activity. In that respect Richey's volume is congruent with new studies in mentality, in popular history, in discourse analysis, and the like.

In yet another step toward a fuller understanding of the religious dimensions of early American Methodism, Richey charts the ways in which the annual conference evolved from the days when it served multiple purposes—both evangelism and organization—to a time when, following the spread of the camp meeting, it became a gathering occupied principally with business concerns. Evangelism, formerly a central intent of the conference, was transferred to the protracted camp meeting. Richey joins others who have written about evangelicalism by demonstrating that early Methodist meetings provided Americans with an alternative to the hierarchical paternalism of the established churches, particularly that of Anglicanism. He shows that the egalitarian tone of Methodism stemmed in great part from the experiential affirmations of its evangelicalism. Richey charts other changes in the story, too, for example, the switch within early American Methodism from antislavery views to the acceptance of holding slaves, and the movement from a more communal ethos to an increasingly radical individualism. In his analysis of all of these developments, he draws upon the clues provided by the different languages employed within the Methodist community.

After reading this volume, it will not be easy for the reader to forget the meaning of various Methodist idioms—"melting," Zion, conference, to name but three. Perhaps the most intriguing image in this collection of essays is that derived from Francis Asbury, that of the "glass" held to the heart. Richey explains this trope in terms of its transparency and the insight it allows into the early Methodist view of the nation. Readers of this volume will have an opportunity to test for themselves the variety of possible meanings—a clear, transparent glass, a looking-glass, a seerstone. Each possesses attractive hermeneutical possibilities.

We hope that *Early American Methodism* will become a model for scholars who wish to explore the *religious* history of other denominations. Every tradition has its own equally revealing vernacular. The worlds of religious discourse created by distinctive language and nuance, whatever the traditions, invite close examination. In Richey's essays we see the interpretive possibilities of creative historical reconstruction.

Catherine L. Albanese
Stephen J. Stein
Series Editors

Introduction

This volume focuses on the earliest years of American Methodism, really from 1770 to 1810. Though each chapter undertakes a distinct inquiry into this phase of the Methodist movement, they interconnect and rely upon one another, share a set of concerns about that period, operate with common assumptions and perspectives, and endeavor to revise long-standing assessments of Methodist development. As the titles indicate, this is self-consciously a revisionist endeavor.

Continuity and change are issues over which these essays agonize. In so exploring Methodist development, each raises the hermeneutical question. What categories serve to exhibit the nature of early Methodism and the changes through which it went? What conceptual framework, what language of analysis serves best? Here this volume takes a decided preference for what might be termed a Methodist vernacular, a language of self-presentation to be found in the literature generated by the movement. That language, so it is argued, best exposes the Methodist experience. But it was not the only Methodist language and certainly not the one typically employed in historical explanation. In fact, Methodists struggled with four distinct languages. Their central problem was that of living with these languages, accommodating them to one another, translating among them. Language vexed Methodist loyalty to the past and adjustment to change.

Change

This book resists the notion, a common one, that Methodism underwent its single and most important change in 1784 at the organizing Christmas Conference. While the significance of that foundational, organizational event is acknowledged, the volume argues strenuously for important continuities between the first and subsequent decades of Methodist experience. And it also points toward a far more dramatic and wrenching change in Methodism in the early nineteenth century, one that did not happen in the short space of a week, could not happen in a single conference, but took place at different rates in different places, permitting residual aspects of this early Methodism to shape experience through much of the nineteenth century.

That early nineteenth century change had several faces to it. One was the loss of innocence, a kind of fall of Methodism. As these chapters show, early Methodism had an Edenic quality to it. It was a troubled Eden, to be sure, but an Eden nonetheless. In what they later termed "the garden of Methodism,"[1] among the peoples of the middle colonies and upper south, Methodist preachers planted a very radical word, one that called for brethren to live together in unity, as sinners freed by Christ and empowered by him to a new, ordered existence spelled out in rule and given form through Methodist structures. The radical character of that word took most dramatic expression in the acceptance accorded Blacks into the Methodist fold. Methodists offered an ambiguous, incomplete acceptance that very early had racist and segregationist aspects. Yet they did invite Blacks into membership, preached freedom, and demanded that members emancipate their slaves. As his first act after conversion, Freeborn Garrettson freed his slaves.[2] Thereafter, he preached abolition. Freedom from sin and freedom from slavery belonged together, so early Methodists thought. However, they retreated rather quickly from such antislavery ideas. That retreat represented an important feature of Methodist loss of innocence and a very important change in the Methodist economy.

The innocence of early Methodist reform (including antislavery) is the concern of several chapters, particularly "Views of the Nation: A Glass to the Heart." That chapter endeavors to show the Edenic quality of Methodism's perception of the social order and efforts at reform. Methodists spoke with fervor, with eschatological urgency, about society and its renewal. Such prophetic utterance was uncalculated, unpolitical. In part, this very innocence proved its undoing. As Methodism took its place in society, it had to calculate its commitments and put them in order. The cost of antislavery proved high, too high for Methodism to sustain. But the cost of giving it up proved high as well. In surrendering this egalitarianism, Methodism lost something of itself. To understand early Methodism is to reckon with the Edenic quality of its commitments, the agonies of its moral dilemmas, and the bitter self-knowledge that their resolution afforded. For Methodists, as for many religious movements, growth and development may look like progress and success from some angles but appear retrogressive and ambiguous from others.

Another Edenic aspect of early Methodism and another casualty of its early nineteenth century change was the richly communal and spiritual character of its organized life. Each chapter, but in different ways, explores the communal-spiritual intensity of Methodist existence and the agonies of its transformation. Serious students of early Methodism acknowledge this communal character. Yet the contrary impression that early Methodism was individualistic and inward in its orientation remains very prevalent. To counter that impression and explore its community, these chapters utilize the language and structures of early Methodism. One such term and one measure of Methodism's communal intensity were the fraternal bonds among the preachers (as well as among the people and between preachers and people). Fraternity receives attention in several chapters.

Fraternity is one of several illustrations employed to indicate the harmony early Methodists sought between means and ends, structures and their purposes, business and religiosity. Methodists put a high premium on Christian brotherhood (and sisterhood). This, too, serves as index of the Edenic quality of Methodism and a measure of its fall. Fraternity proved difficult to sustain. It could even yield fratricide. Fraternity did not fall with one blow. Methodists did not simply replicate, typologically, the first Eden's fraternity (though some early Methodists found among their peers an actor for Cain and ample cause for his murder). Fraternity continued. Indeed, well down into the twentieth century Methodists of various denominations would speak, with seriousness, about the ministerial order as a brotherhood. Yet fraternities do change. And the change experienced through and in Methodist fraternity in the early nineteenth century was important. To monitor that change several of the chapters examine the structure of fraternity—the conference—and chart early stages of its evolution.

Continuities

Certain aspects of early nineteenth century change in Methodism are illustrated by continuities that have been insufficiently explored. One that is under scrutiny at several points in these pages has to do with conference, the basic structure of Methodist governance. Between conference (both annual and quarterly) and the camp meeting a continuity exists which, when properly understood, illustrates important dimensions of Methodist development. These essays show that quarterly meetings and annual conferences functioned in a revivalistic mode and frequently had a revivalistic impact on the communities in which they were held. Conferences served as what would later be known as 'protracted meetings' and lacked primarily the tents of the camp meeting. The important continuity, however, was not of form but of substance. The revivalist substance, so it is argued, was transferred from conference to camp meeting. In consequence, conferences began a long evolution into administrative/legislative/judicial entities. Conference's shift from revival to business was, then, facilitated by the emergence of the camp meeting as a kind of conference surrogate, which by carrying on conference's spiritual functions left conference to do business. The continuity between conference and camp meeting actually and ironically facilitated an important discontinuity or change within Methodism's basic structure, the conference.

Another continuity which takes several ironic turns is the subject of the fourth chapter, "The Southern Accent of American Methodism." Methodism took its shape, so it is argued, from the ethos of the upper south, really the Chesapeake. And many of its characteristic concerns and features are rooted in those southern experiences. However, for a variety of interesting reasons, Methodists (conveniently) forgot that connection between the national Methodist movement and its southern origins. The recovery of that particular continuity helps explain important aspects of Methodist behavior, as for instance its ambiguous and ambivalent treatment of Blacks.

Not often forgotten is the continuity between John Wesley and America, between the earlier British and American phases of the movement. Indeed, because they stress that connection, Methodist historians often preoccupy themselves with explaining how, when, and why American Methodists broke the bonds with Mr. Wesley. Methodist historiography concerns itself with Americanization, a fetish shared with interpreters of American religion and American history.[3] At what point or in what developments did the movement come out from under Wesley's authority? When did the American church assert its identity and character? What constituted indigenization? To these questions, often the Christmas Conference of 1784 supplies the answer. That organizing gathering of Methodism serves as the convenient transition between British/colonial and American phases of the movement. On one side of that date is 'society within the Church of England under the governance of Wesley' and on the other side is independent church. In these pages and especially in the fifth essay, "Conference as a Means of Grace," this interpretation moves in both directions away from 1784. On the one hand, there were more prolonged continuities between the British conference and the Methodist conferences, continuities that extended well past 1784. On the other hand, the indigenizing process began earlier, essentially with Methodist plantation on these shores, and proceeded steadily through and beyond 1784. American Methodism, then, remained 'provincial' long after 1784 but had been indigenizing long before. Several chapters, in addition to this one, resist the notion that this process is easily subsumed under a category like 'Americanization'. The dependence upon Britain lasted through much of the nineteenth century; the changes that effected much of the indigenization had something to do with deliberate and ideational commitments like democracy and nationalism but also derived from religious dynamics that occasioned subtle changes in the texture of patterns otherwise unchanged from Mr. Wesley's stipulations and strikingly similar to current British practice; distance and growth and events and new problems prompted much of the deliberate change; and, as already mentioned, and explored at some length in "The Southern Accent," the important initial orientation to America had a very regional aspect to it. This is not to deny Methodism a role in democratization and nation-building. Nathan Hatch has correctly located Methodism among those chaotic and aggressive movements that exploded out from the Revolution to evangelize the American peoples.[4] Yet, he also notes how ambiguously Methodists participated in those trends, being a force for democratization and proponents of an egalitarian gospel while building a singularly undemocratic, episcopal, and preacher-dominated polity. So Americanization perhaps should not be the first term of resort. It still may be very useful, but perhaps for less broad-stroked purposes.

The Terms for Historical Explanation

If 'Americanization' should be utilized with more care, how about other standard explanations of Methodist development, as, for instance, its movement from society to church or the more sociological rendering of that, from sect to denomination? On such constructs these chapters also express a cautionary note. As in the case of Americanization, these notions suffer from being overworked and insufficiently attended. Like any draft animal they can be abused. These chapters, in fact, explore the dynamics that the notions of society-to-church or sect-to-denomination (or church) cover but carefully avoid using them.[5] The essays singly and the volume as a whole endeavor to exhibit the nature of early Methodism and the changes through which it went. In so doing, they employ terms that recur through Methodist speech and writing but which have not frequently been used for historical explanation. Fraternity is one. Zion, melting, dancing, the continent, conference, quarterly meeting, journals, and history are other terms that we use to image the movement and explain its development.

Chapter 3's subtitle "A Glass to the Heart" serves similar purposes.

Francis Asbury employed this curious image to invite the reader to see what he took to heart, what he valued most. In my chapter, it serves to represent the politically ambiguous and eschatological character of Methodist reform and social ethics. Such rubrics are not intended so much as replacements for more conventional explanatory terms as ways of refreshing explanation. The purpose of the volume will be well served if by these reconceptualizations readers gain fresh insight into early Methodism and can take that insight to its literature or other historical treatments.

The Adequacy of Methodist Language

A related concern, already touched upon, has to do with the adequacy of denominational language. All essays argue that Methodism suffered from a complex of problems rooted in the imprecision of the Methodist language(s). Much of the difficulty derived from the plurality of languages with which Methodists worked and the babel that resulted.[6] This is a passing concern in most of the essays, the explicit concern of the first and last.

The first language, Methodists did not 'own' but shared with other pietists or evangelicals. It was the vernacular of religious experience, a richly biblical and highly evocative language. The Spirit would 'fall' upon a meeting. In it, people had 'melting' experiences, 'found great freedom', felt themselves knit together in 'love', called one another 'brother', 'rejoiced in the prosperity of Zion' and defended its walls against the forces of Satan. Such terminology derived from the revival and its defining experience, conversion. The First Great Awakening made it a folk idiom, shared across denominational boundaries, available and malleable for Methodists and subsequent evangelical movements. Methodists found it highly compatible with their own, a second or Wesleyan language. So Methodists employed it on the stump, in their journals, and in their publications.[7] Yet, it never found its way into the canon of Methodism.[8]

Methodists' received language and distinguishing tongue came from the Wesleys. Methodists spoke of class, society, itinerancy, circuits, holiness, preachers, stewards, leaders, tickets, love feast, quarterly meeting, conference. Membership carried its privileges. It also required the mastery of this new language. Many doubtless knew it only in its oral form. For the dictionary and grammar thereof, Methodists turned to the functioning constitutions of Methodism, the British *Large Minutes* and after 1784 its replacement, the *Discipline*. This language and its power to shape Methodist life are the concern of the fifth essay. Like the vernacular it conveyed a vital religious meaning.[9] Tensions developed between these two languages (vernacular and Wesleyan), as several of the essays show. That tension shapes one entire chapter, "From Quarterly to Camp Meeting," which compares the official "quarterly meeting" with the vernacular "camp meeting."

In 1784, Methodists formally adopted a third language. For purposes of simplicity we might term it an episcopal language. It came with John Wesley's blessing and largely from his hand. Most American Methodists found its terms and cadences familiar since Wesley borrowed it (with certain revisions and excisions) from the Church of England. With this language, Methodists spoke of deacons, elders, and bishops, gave themselves ecclesial and sacramental legitimacy, and added significant structures and procedures to their organized life. Most would hear it only on sacramental occasions or when Methodists debated critics from other denominations. But for all its familiarity and despite its importance as a way of conferring ecclesial identity and stature on what had been ostensibly a reform movement within Anglicanism, this language proved difficult to integrate with the first two. In one way or another, all of the essays derive their narrative from that tension.[10] How could Methodists express the height and depth of their religious experience in the formal cadences of Anglicanism? That had been the generating question of the (British) Wesleyan movement; now it had become the constitutional problem of American Methodism.[11]

A fourth language came into prominence somewhat later in the Methodist saga, toward the mid-nineteenth century. An American political idiom, this republican language we know in the Declaration of Independence, the Constitution, the Federalist papers, stump speeches, and political party platforms. It became the repository of American hopes, beliefs, and commitments. As the religion of the republic, it made its claims on denominations as well as individuals and elicited counter-claims in turn.[12] The interplay between traditional, Judeo-Christian and public religion occurred in many arenas—from the spotlighted presidency and supreme court out to dim-lit dramas in virtually every public forum throughout the land—and invariably made American values an issue in denominational life and traditional values an issue in public life.

These pages and particularly "Views of the Nation" propose that early Methodists made less use of this fourth language than has often been thought. The main branch of the Methodists came to terms with republican values much later, as an important part of its adjustment to American society. To be sure, early Methodism did spawn a reformist effort which self-consciously appropriated the democratic and republican language and sought to transform Methodist authority in accordance with those values. Calling itself Republican Methodists, this group followed James

O'Kelly in demanding that the movement apply to itself the lessons of
American Independence. That revolt tested Methodist commitment to its
other languages. Most Methodists chose to follow Asbury and reject the
Republican cause. Their values and behavior are intelligible when conceived in terms of the first three and particularly the first two language
systems outlined here. Furthermore, the schism of those "Republican
Methodists" actually rendered more problematic subsequent Methodist
endeavor to incorporate American republican values and perhaps made
inevitable the later separation of the Methodist Protestants, who also
raised within the church a democratic banner. Neither of these reform
efforts receives attention in this chapter. Methodism's popular character
is not neglected, though. Instead, it is seen in terms of different languages.[13] The populist values of early Methodism, this book argues, pul-
sate through the vernacular it spoke so easily.

A Vernacular Explanation

The whole volume might also be understood in those terms. It is a
vernacular reading of Methodist history. It attempts to explain the nature
and development of Methodism through its first two languages and especially the first. Among Methodism's four languages, we have privileged the
Pietist idiom that pitted the citizens of Zion against the dark forces of
Satan. The adoption of this language as normative does provide us an
interesting vantage on Methodist developments. That vocabulary allows
us, as already indicated, to read Methodism afresh; to recapture some of
the nuance of Methodist experience; to expose the dilemmas Methodists
faced as they struggled to translate that experience into the languages
known by the world; to recognize their agonies in attempting to live with a
plurality of languages; and perhaps to view as inevitable the losses they
accepted as they settled into a world where the episcopal language and
the American vernacular prevailed.

Invariably, a revisionist effort such as this tends toward one-sidedness.
By taking the Methodist vernacular on its own terms and employing it for
explanatory purposes, the volume accepts some distortions and imbal-
ances as the cost of vigor and freshness in a new reading. A full account
will go beyond this. It will need to take the angle of vision of each language, of all four languages, into account. Each of these four, after all, was
a language of Methodism. Each offered an intelligible version of what it
meant to be Methodist. For each, there emerged scribes, linguists, interpreters, lexicographers. Through these champions, each vied for primacy

as *the* Methodist language. Accordingly, historical assessments can be and indeed have been rendered from each linguistic vantage.

Here, then, one language is used to portray Methodism's entire linguistic world. That has been done self-consciously. Indeed, at many points our endeavor has been to contrast and compare Methodism's languages. Yet, some readers may wish to turn to more 'balanced' or conventional readings for reference. At the least, that will provide other terms for what is here portrayed.

This volume, after all, has not employed familiar words, even for its titles. "Conference as a Means of Grace" treats what in more conventional terms might be called the polity or conference structure of Methodism. "Community, Fraternity, and Order" deals with ministry, including episcopacy. "Views of the Nation: A Glass to the Heart" examines Methodism's much vaunted reform spirit, its ethic. "From Quarterly to Camp Meeting" studies revivals and revivalism. And "The Southern Accent of American Methodism" concerns Methodism's self-understanding, self-image, and historical self-estimate. The several chapters thus cover much of the Methodist economy. They do so in what, it is hoped, the reader will find an interesting fashion.

EARLY
AMERICAN
METHODISM

1. Community, Fraternity, and Order

Monday, 3. Our quarterly meeting began, and brother Shadford preached on the subject of the barren fig-tree. On *Tuesday* we held our love feast at nine, and I preached at twelve. brethren Owing, Samuel Spraggs, and Shadford, all spoke. There were many friends from Virginia, and the congregation was very large. It was a powerful, melting time, and concluded in the spirit of love. . . .

Monday, 10. We set out for the quarterly meeting at Deer Creek. On *Tuesday* our love feast began at ten, and at half-past two I began the public exercise, from Heb. XIII, 17, 18, "Obey them that have the rule over you, and submit yourselves: for they watch for your souls as they that must give account, that they may do it with joy, and not with grief; for this is unprofitable for you. Pray with us: for we trust we have a good conscience, in all things willing to live honestly." The preachers were stationed without any trouble; and all was done in harmony and love.[1]

These two November 1777 entries from Francis Asbury's journal summarize early American Methodism's idea of its experience: a community of love, nourished by a fraternity of the word, ordered in conference. In sustaining that reading of these Asbury passages we propose:

that community, fraternity, and order characterized early Methodist ecclesial experience;

that Methodist religious experience demanded fresh terms, an idiom generated out of the religious life itself but evocative of Scripture as well;

that this vernacular presupposed and actually flowed from the routines and rhythms of the Wesleyan movement, a movement which had already elaborated its own grammar of the Christian life;

that the vernacular and Wesleyan languages existed in creative tension, giving a movement run on authoritarian and hierarchical (albeit rather unpretentiously hierarchical) bases a popular and egalitarian appeal;

that on this creative tension, the church imposed in 1784, when it formally organized itself, an episcopal idiom, adopted to give legitimacy to and make ecclesial sense of the religious life that Methodism had sustained;

and that this particular Pentecost—the juxtaposition of three idioms and particularly the imposition of episcopal terminology on the dynamisms of early Methodism—yielded a linguistic cacophony that Methodists may have never adequately decoded.

Community in Early American Methodism

Consider Jesse Lee's description of a quarterly meeting in Sussex County, Virginia, on a late July weekend in 1787.

> This meeting was favoured with more of the divine presence than any other that had been known before. The sight of the mourners was enough to penetrate the most careless heart. The divine power was felt among the people before the preachers came together. Many of the young converts from the quarterly meeting that had been held two days before at Mabry's had come together, and uniting with other Christians in singing and praying, the heavenly fire had begun to kindle, and the flame of love and holy zeal was spreading among the people, which caused them to break out in loud praises to God. Some when they met would hang on each other, or embrace each other in their arms, and weep aloud, and praise the Lord with all their might. The sight of those who were thus overwhelmed with the love and presence of God, would cause sinners to weep and tremble before the Lord.
>
> By the time the preachers came within half a mile of the chapel, they heard the people shouting and praising God. When they came up they found numbers weeping, both in the chapel and in the open air. Some were on the ground crying for mercy, and others in extacies of joy.[2]

Interpretations of this "remarkable revival of religion" typically grasp at the emotion of the people and the power of the preaching. Neither can be denied. Both were important in the continuation and intensification of this revival. But an interesting fact deserves comment. The community experienced "the divine power" and presence by meeting together prior to the preachers' arrival. Lee had remarked in surprise of a preparatory prayer meeting—"souls were frequently converted at those meetings, even when there was no preacher present." This revival, then, was preeminently a communal affair. The emotion that Lee catalogued was social or interpersonal in character. Persons engaged one another—singing, praying, shouting, praising God, weeping. These were communal acts. The interaction and intimacy and sense of oneness which Wesley expected of his small religious groups, the class and band, had gone public. The deeply felt, affective unity expressed itself in love—of course to God but most dramatically toward one another. For early Methodists, community was itself intensely spiritual, contagiously so, a spreading fire of love and holy zeal. That communal intensity expressed itself physically in emotional embracing and visually, even for the newcomer, in the displays and expressions of affection.

Methodists had a word for such intense community, a very intriguing and suggestive term: melting. For a 1779 quarterly meeting Asbury scribbled: "Our love feast[3] began at nine, and public worship at twelve o'clock. The operations of the Holy Spirit were very powerful in the congregation; so that there was a general melting." On a Frederick quarterly meeting two years earlier he remarked: "the next day our meeting began with a love feast; and we had a powerful melting time."[4] 'Melting', commonly used in Methodist journals and diaries (if the occasion demanded), is not an entry in theological lexicons, either of early or twentieth-century Methodism. Clearly Methodists reached for, groped for, terms adequate to their experience of community. Thomas Rankin caught the ineffability of community:

> At ten, our general love feast began. There were such a number of white and blacks as never had attended on such an occasion before. After we had sung and prayed, the cloud burst from my mind, and the power of the Lord descended in such an extraordinary manner as I had never seen since my landing at Philadelphia. All the preachers were so overcome with the Divine presence, that they could scarce address the people; but only in broken accents saying: "This is none other than the house of God and the gate of heaven." When any of the people stood up to declare the loving kindness of God, they were so overwhelmed with the Divine presence that they were obliged to sit down and let the silence speak his praise. . . . For about three hours the gale of the spirit thus continued to break upon the dry bones, and they did live, the life of glorious love."

Still at a loss for words, Rankin concluded doxologically, "All glory be to God on high, and to the Lamb that sits on the throne, forever and forever."[5]

As the previous citations indicate, community expressed itself most intensely in the love feast. Freeborn Garrettson captured its character by inverting word order. He spoke of "a comfortable feast of love."[6] That it was, a community feasting on love, an inward sharing of one another. Here individuals gave themselves by offering what was most privately, personally their own—their own story. In love feasts, Methodists related their religious experience. In verbal surrender, they bonded themselves to one another, to the Methodist society, and, in their view, to Christ. The formula continues to work in Alcoholics Anonymous and other twelve step organizations. These shared experiences, when reduced to writing and in two hundred years' perspective, do have a certain formulary quality. That may or may not have been even evident to simple people, many speaking publicly for the first time, all struggling to share in words what words could not say. William Watters reported of a love feast he attended:

> I . . . believe Heaven above will differ more in quantity than in quality. Never did I hear such experiences before. Our eyes overflowed with tears, and our hearts with love to God and each other. The holy fire, the heavenly flame, spread wider and wider, and rose higher and higher. O! happy people whose God is the Lord, may none of you ever weary in well doing.[7]

Community was deeply experienced, and ritualized in love feast. It was also well institutionalized. The most day-to-day, week-to-week forms are familiar Methodist structures. The classes, societies, preaching sustained Methodist community within the neighborhoods in which people lived. However, the most dramatic, public, expression of community was that two-day event within which love feasts commonly occurred and which both Asbury and Lee described. In quarterly meeting Methodism offered itself as a new community, a social alternative to the broken community of the world. And it quite literally acted out its invitation to come—a dramatic engagement of community with world. The action began the first day, preferably Saturday, by the community withdrawing to order itself—in circuit business and preaching. The next morning began with love feast which nonmembers could attend "only twice or thrice."[8] As the day progressed, events became more public. By that staging, Methodists moved the drama into and enveloped the audience. Before 1784, the day was essentially filled with what they termed "public preaching" and exhorting.

After 1784, a typical pattern was love feast at 9:00, communion at 11:00, public preaching at 12:00. Memorial services, marriages, baptisms followed or interspersed as appropriate. In a Chesapeake society which defined community by event rather than place, where community quite literally occurred at dance, horse-race, cock-fight, election, Methodists in quarterly meeting modeled and offered a new form of community. In quarterly meeting, Methodism aimed to become its gospel of free grace, with the universalism of Christian love engaging the world. Appropriately, these were often large affairs. Freeborn Garrettson reported crowds of 1,000 at love feast and twice that at public meeting. On Sunday of the Bolinbroke Quarterly Meeting, August 19 and 20, 1780, Garrettson claimed, "It appeared as if the whole country came together at 11:00 o'clock. I think at least there was between two and three thousand. Four of us preached and one exhorted. Glory be to God, Bolinbroke never saw such a day before. I think the devil's kingdom was well shaken." [9]

The numbers may conjure up the anonymity of twentieth-century mass revivalism. Such an impression would be mistaken, for in the Chesapeake such gatherings were commonplace. Events defined community and brought together persons already bonded by similar events. Their ties of previous kinship varied—blood, marriage, commerce, debt, class, sport, religion, ownership. In quarterly meeting, Methodists repudiated such worldly kinship. Instead, Methodists countered with a new kinship, a new form of community. They symbolized the radical, world-transforming character of new kinship and new community by including slaves. James Meacham termed them "my Dear Black Brethren." [10] Other preachers spoke in similar kinship terms. Such an assertion, in a slave society, in a society which boasted its patriarchy, was a prophetic act. It proclaimed judgment on the kinship and order of the world and offered a new way of living together. Slaves to Christ, Methodists loved one another and all humanity. To honor the world's code of slavery, to honor the world's pattern of kinship, was to reject that of Christ. In him were all brothers and sisters. Methodism so understood itself as community. A second Methodist value gave special meaning and authority to the term 'brother'.

Fraternity

The Methodist community offered its Christ, but in so doing offered itself, to the world. The invitation was free. That Arminian badge Methodists wore with pride. Grace flowed free. Accepting that free invitation Methodists knew proved costly, for acceptance entailed repudiating the order of the world in favor of the new order of Methodism. To that 'order' we will return later in the chapter. Acceptance also entailed drawing lines, creating boundaries. Fraternity affirmed and sealed those boundaries.

The most important boundary we have already treated, namely that between Methodism and the world. The terms 'brother' and 'sister' distinguished those with whom one shared intense Christian bonds from those with whom one did not. In current ecclesiastical usage and particularly in comic routines thereon the terms are used indiscriminately. For early Methodism the contrary was the case. The journals of the period evidence the selective employment of the terms, as we shall see. That very selectivity accented Methodism's radical spiritual egalitarianism. 'Brother' and 'sister' shattered the lines drawn by the world—lines of race, class, family, language—by drawing a new line between Methodism and the world. Hence fraternity (or perhaps we should say fraternity and sorority) in one sense, its most important sense, divided Methodism from the world.

However, fraternity also divided Methodism internally. The lines that it drew within may have been carried partly by intonation or emphasis, for the term continued to bear its egalitarian sense even when it violated that egalitarianism. Yet the term 'brother', in particular, allowed the distinctions of the world to creep back in. Classes, for instance, were often of one race, as well as, we might add, of one sex. And when 'brother' was used in that internally divisive way, it gave peculiar counter-significance to terms used by those excluded. Hence the word 'sister' came to bear quite important meanings among women that we are only now beginning to recover. Similarly, the word 'brother' among Black Christians has incredibly rich overtones that counter the restrictive use of the term by whites.

Here, though, another very important divisive use of the term 'brother' deserves scrutiny.[11] On a trip in 1789 Richard Whatcoat, already nominated to the episcopacy but only later elected, noted:

Augt 1—1789 F asbury Bror willis & I Rode to Cornal Barrotts   F asbury preached   I exhorted

2 Rode to Jos Cressups C[hapel]   F asbury preached   I Exhorted   Bror Willes Spoke from Nathanie[l]   The word was with weight   May it be lasting

. . .

16 Bror Willis Re[a]d the Servis   I preach & also at A rchible Wiggens at three & Bror Haggerty Exhorted   Bror Willis preach & Bror adams at the Springs in the afternoon &C   Truly it appears that [like] Light & darkness the Children of God & the Children of the wicked Can have But Little fellowship together

[Oct]

17 Rode to Dover opened the Q Meeting   Bror Asbury preach a
Great sermon   Bror Everit & Bror Moor Exhorted &c Bror
Everit preach in the Evning &C

Octr 18–1789 Lovefeast Began About halfpas[t] Eight   I & Brors
Ratclif[and] Boyour Exhorted   Bror Asbury prayed &C &C the
Lord was powerfuly presant   Jacob Brush and Wm Jesup were
ordained Elders   Bishop asbury preached A Great Sermon   I exhorted   Bror Everit preachd &C—I preached in
the Evning at Mr. Basits Esq[12]

Whom did Whatcoat call brother? Here not the laity. And only after a couple of months of traveling together would Whatcoat confide in his own journal that Asbury was his brother. Asbury, on whose head Whatcoat had laid his hands in ordination! With whom he had labored five years! Whatcoat reserved "brother" for his fellow preachers. Brother signified a very special relation within the body of preachers. Preachers addressed one another routinely as "brother." To be sure, Whatcoat was not consistent in limiting 'brother' to the preachers. With others he used the terms brother and sister to designate Methodists generally. Still the term took on special force when applied to those who traveled together.

Something of that is captured in the letters to Edward Dromgoole, Irish-born itinerant, who was admitted to trial in 1774, traveled until 1786, settled as a local preacher, and virtually kept inn for Methodist preachers. Rueben Ellis wrote in 1786: "My dear Brother. My unabating Love to you, moved me, tho at this distance to write—Being persuaded also that you would be glad to know how I fare!"[13] John Hagerty in a letter dated the following year began:

My Dear Brother.
   Grace, mercy & peace be multiplied to you & yours, altho I have been long silent, & have not wrote to you, I have not forgot you but as ever do feel a cordial affection for you, & wish you all happiness in this & the world to come, hope you keep your head above water and are going on your way to the Kingdom, laying aside weight and urging your way straight forward.

He concluded, "accept this as a token of love and believe me to (be) your affectionate Friend & Bror in Christ."[14] And John Dickins in 1788, "My Dear and much Esteemed [Friend], Dont think, I love but little because I write but seldom."[15] Perhaps the letters lent themselves to false sentimentality? Consider the notations that James Meacham made for himself in his journal. They indicate how such letters were received. "May 26, 1792, rode to Hanover Town to meet with my Elder bro J.E. who brought in several Letters from Sundry Brothers, we had sweet union while Together, my soul thinks it a great blessing to be with the Elder Brethren & the Preachers." Two years earlier he had jotted: "Sweet is the Company of the preachers."[16]

Like community, fraternity was deeply felt. Yet it was not simply affect. Brotherhood was well institutionalized. The institutionalizations—itinerancy and conference—deserve comparison with the myriad forms of fraternity known today: voluntary association, work unit, old school tie, senatorial courtesy, sports camaraderie, profession, shared crisis experience, common allegiance, ideology, missional bonds. Methodists had these and more. Even so, the deep feelings that these Methodist itinerants had for one another, the texture of those relationships, the inner world of that fraternity may be imperfectly represented by twentieth-century male bonding. Fraternity clearly has eroded, is actually highly suspect, in ecclesial settings today. The role or professional dimensions of ministry, the organizational and political aspects of conference, the presence and prominence of women make the continued use of 'brother' a kind of archaism, a quaint form of address. In a Methodist gathering today when the chair recognizes "The brother from Baltimore," listeners readily conclude that the chair does not know the speaker's name. Today's irony masks yesterday's dynamism. Fraternity was critical to the life of early Methodism.

Its most important form may be the most difficult to recover. The popular image of itinerancy is that conveyed by the famous picture of the circuit rider, the solitary, cloaked horseman, braving storm and cold, in midstream, pressing on, face guarded from the elements, to deliver the gospel. The circuit rider symbolized individual will, great fortitude, and singleness of purpose. The picture that emerges from journals of eighteenth-century preachers is different. It is implied in the two-word notation *"We rode."* What is impressive is how often the preachers rode together, how often they contrived to be together. The intense affection felt for one another derived from networking, from sharing the itinerant life, from behaving like brothers. The traveling together would not be unexpected of Asbury who as bishop was guided through the connection by the local leadership and typically had an entourage. But we find the same pattern for the ordinary traveling preachers who, at the close of the day, noted down who preached and who exhorted. They had a word for it that like so much else has been turned into an organization, yokefellows.

Yoking, fraternity—like natural brotherhood—was given in birth, actually the new birth (conversion they called it), and grown into. Stith Mead detailed the various dimensions of this relationship. It began while he was 'under conviction'.

> I providentially fell in with the Rev. Christopher S. Mooring, a Methodist Circuit Preacher, and rode in company with him the same evening, about fifteen mile, to Mr. William Read's—in this travel with the Rev. C.S.M., I received some wholesome instruction on experimental and practical religion. On our arrival at Mr. Read's we found there had been preaching the same day there by Rev. R. Pope, and Rev. John Ayers to help him—a part of the congregations having delayed, the meeting was resumed in the afternoon, first by a warm exhortation by Rev. J.A.—secondly by Rev. C.S.M.—and thirdly by the Rev. R. Pope.
>
> I rode with the Methodist preachers to preaching at Callaways School-house. The congregation was so large, the People could not all get into the house.[17]

After conversion he noted: "I rode with Rev. C. S. Mooring to Liberty, Bedford court-house, and heard him preach—". Upon joining the Methodists he recorded:

> I employed some time travelling with the preachers round Bedford Circuit, particularly the Rev. R. P., preacher in charge, to acquaint myself with the Methodist *discipline* and *doctrine*. This brought me to examine for the first time, the subject of negro slavery, and found some struggles of the mind, before I could fully give up the idea of possessing them in some shape or other—having been raised and educated in expectation of holding them. But the more I examined the subject impartially in print, and conversing with individuals, the greater evil I discovered, until I fully gave up the principle of negro slavery.[18]

Mead was inducted into a traveling brotherhood. Pope converted him and became his 'big' brother. Elsewhere in the narrative, Mead indicated that after his conversion he became disillusioned. An unbrotherly Presbyterian nourished that discouragement. He challenged the authenticity of the conversion when Mead could not articulate the meaning of it in satisfactory terms. Mead "felt some encouragement" under a Baptist preacher. But when he returned to hear the Methodist, Mr. Pope: "I had not been under the sound of his voice but a few minutes, before I felt very happy; the love of God, and love to all mankind increased as I sat on a seat." The traveling brotherhood tutored Mead in the faith, brought him into the Methodist ethos, infused him with new values. Within this fellowship of the road, Mead eventually trained as a preacher. Traveling with other preachers permitted observation, practice, modeling, criticism, support.

How direct or indirect the counsel, how intentional or accidental this seminary on horseback, we perhaps cannot know. We catch only the residue of it in the critical asides the preachers made about one another's preaching.

The religious dimensions of this traveling brotherhood have been represented by the fervid commitment preachers held to itinerancy. To the prediction of his settling James Meacham protested (to himself, in his *Journal*): "I hope I shall die a travelling preacher."[19] But why such an attachment to traveling, what was the spiritual core of itinerancy? Was it mobility? Moving rapidly around on horse? Changing appointments at three months, six months; a year, two years? Or was it rather what mobility facilitated—an intense bonding, analogous only to familial ties, in loyalty to the highest ideal known, service to the Word? Marriage threatened the bond, and location—the designation in the Methodist *Discipline* for those who relinquished the traveling relation—fouled its engine. Asbury wanted celibates, and healthy ones. Marriage, farming, ill health—all these clearly damaged itinerancy. They have induced interpreters to focus upon the physical, material aspects of the shared office, but it was the sharing that really mattered. Meacham caught the religious dimensions of fraternity with an oft-used phrase, "sweet Christian conference." That covered the gathering of several ministers, a quarterly meeting, engagement with a single minister.[20] Meacham's phrase points us to the second important institutionalization of fraternity.

On the occasions that preachers gathered—quarterly meetings and annual conferences—separated yokefellows were reunited. These were communal occasions, as we have seen. These were times of order, as we shall see. But these were fraternal events as well. Preachers' journals, for instance, explicitly named the brothers at quarterly meeting, their roles and performances.[21] Both quarterly meetings and annual conferences were deeply emotional experiences. They were occasions for agony as well as affection. Conflict, debate, leave-taking, discipline, divided brothers. One poignant scene occurred during the Revolution when the British preachers departed leaving Asbury and the Americans. Some felt similar agony at another departure, when James O'Kelly walked out with those who called themselves Republican Methodists.

> He has taken his fare well of conference. I think my poor heart scarcely ever felt the like before, I could not refrain from weeping deeply I hope God will still direct aright, & give us our dear old bro. & yokefellow back again—if he comes not back, I fear bad consequences will accrue.[22]

The divisions were felt so keenly because of what brothers did together—converse, work, learn, legislate, administer, hear the Word, experience love feast and sacrament, and perhaps most important, listen to one another relate their religious journey and describe their labors, in terms of which conference judged effectiveness. Methodism symbolized these commonalities with a uniform pay scale and appointment timetable. Methodism saw itself as a community of love nourishing and nourished by a fraternity of the Word.

Order

Methodism also saw itself as a new order. And the quarterly meetings and annual conferences became occasions for the ministry to order itself, the societies and classes. Discipline concretized order. Methodists recognized that by naming their book *The Discipline.* Order was also symbolized by the assistant (later presiding elder) who presided over quarterly meetings, and by the general assistant (later bishop) who presided over conferences. In these gatherings their presence, the roles they exercised, and the authority they possessed counterposed paternity to fraternity and community. On these occasions, and especially quarterly meetings, the three ideals of Methodism pressed against one another most sharply. The presiding elder assumed primary responsibility for ordering preachers and community; as a fraternity of the Word, the preachers aimed to cultivate the spiritual resources of one another and the people; and the people tried to manifest Methodism's gospel to the world as an ordered community of love.

Conferences acted on behalf of Methodism as a whole but were less representative of the whole they ordered. Only the traveling preachers attended. Yet community still operated as an ideal. Asbury's sometime notation—"all was conducted in peace and love"[23]—conveyed his sense that the ideals balanced. Others did not always size the matter up in that fashion. Asbury himself made very different judgments about the conference of 1774 chaired by Rankin, though both recognized the ideals of order, fraternity, and community at play. Rankin had concluded: "We spoke our minds freely, one to another in love; and whatever we thought would further the work we most cheerfully embraced."[24] Asbury analyzed it differently:

> The overbearing spirit of a certain person had excited my fears. My judgment was stubbornly opposed for a while, and at last submitted to.

But it is my duty to bear all things with a meek and patient spirit. Our conference was attended with great power; and, all things considered, with great harmony.[25]

Asbury's removal from the general superintendency had obviously sharpened his discomfort with Rankin's reordering of Methodism. But exceptional though it be, it illustrates the far more common fraternal unease with the concentration of authority in one of the brothers. Conference occasioned such perceptions because it was at once a fraternal gathering and the time appointed for ordering the connection.

Personification of ordering in the superintendency only heightened that clash. That personification was well illustrated in this later Asbury journal entry:

I will tell the world what I rest my authority upon. 1. Divine authority. 2. Seniority in America. 3. The election of the General Conference. 4. My ordination by Thomas Coke, William Philip Otterbein, German Presbyterian minister, Richard Whatcoat, and Thomas Vasey. 5. Because the signs of an apostle have been seen in me.[26]

Such attitudes explain in part why order did not elicit the ecstasy that community and fraternity commanded. Comparable intensity was often directed *against* order and particularly *against* its personification. Yet order was vital to both community and fraternity. And Methodists acknowledged that in commitment, consent, and submission, as had Asbury to Rankin. In a later statement made with the powers of the episcopacy under attack by James O'Kelly, Asbury made consent to order the central issue. Absenting himself from conference, he wrote:

My dear Brethren:
    Let my absence give you no pain—Dr. Coke presides. I am happily excused from assisting to make laws by which myself am to be governed; I have only to obey and execute. I am happy in the consideration that I never stationed a preacher through enmity, or as a punishment. I have acted for the glory of God, the good of the people, and to promote the usefulness of the preachers. Are you sure, that, if you please yourselves, the people will be as fully satisfied? They often say, "Let us have such a preacher"; and sometimes, "We will not have such a preacher—we will sooner pay him to stay at home." Perhaps, I must say, "his appeal forced him upon you." I am one, ye are many. I am as willing to serve you as ever. I want not to sit in any man's way. I scorn to solicit votes. I am a very trembling, poor creature to hear praise or dispraise. Speak your minds freely; but remember, you are only making laws for the present time. It may be that as in some other

things, so in this, a future day may give you further light. I am yours, &c.

Francis Asbury

dated Baltimore, Maryland, Thursday, 8th, November 1792[27]

To act "for the glory of God, the good of the people, and . . . the usefulness of the preachers," that was the ideal of order. Whether Asbury was as disinterested and faithful in that as he claimed is another matter. The office stood for that ideal. Here was a unifying strength in Methodism—the ordering of the spiritual resources of each for the sake of the whole connection and ultimately the kingdom.

Community, Fraternity, and Order

When Methodism balanced these three ideals, it could possess incredible power. Early Methodism achieved that balance most fully in the quarterly meeting. There in the midst of the world—frequently outdoors or in public space so as to accommodate the crowds—community occurred, responded to the 'word' of the fraternity, and was ordered by elder or superintendent. In quarterly meeting, Methodism most fully displayed its wares and was, in that sense, most fully the church. Appropriately, great revivals occurred. These occasions to care for the circuit's business became festivals for religious renewal. Structure and mission were one, and organization was the means for communal religious experience.

Community actualized in feasts of love, traveling fraternity of the word, order for the glory of God—are these not just new and idealized labels for familiar things? For people, preachers, bishops? Or dimensions of the ministerial prerogatives of sacrament, word, and order? Or three of the structural features of Wesleyanism: first—class, society, and quarterly meeting; second—itinerancy and conference; third—scriptural episcopacy? Or the Methodist expression of the prized mixed constitution of eighteenth-century Britain—democracy, aristocracy, monarchy?

These more conventional designations, of course, remain useful. The familiar terms, however, do not do justice to early Methodism, its nature or its evolution. To illustrate only with the last speculation, yes, Methodism did indeed have a mixed constitution, a balance of democratic, aristocratic, and monarchical principles. Yet these were religious and not simply constitutional or political principles. Methodism labored for love not democracy, for fraternity not the aristocracy of the preachers, for order not the arbitrary will of monarchical episcopacy. And so to portray the agendas born of democracy and fraternity, as for instance O'Kelly's Republican movement, as polity matters only is to miss their deeper significance for Methodists. We need, and O'Kelly needed, adequate terms for the Methodist revolution.

American Methodists had a problem with names. Mead's crisis—of not being able to name what he had experienced—was, in a sense, Methodism's as a whole. Methodists needed terms to describe the religious revolution that had occurred on American shores. The Methodists had provided handsomely for spirituality, in both its interior and communal forms. What they desperately needed were ecclesial terms which made sense of that experience. 'Sweet Christian conference' said it; 'melting' said it. But those terms sufficed only where that vernacular prevailed. They were not the stuff of creeds and confessions.

Wesley's terms also worked—class, society, quarterly meeting, conference, helpers, assistants, etc. That language, in fact, mandated the dynamisms, tasks, belonging, and order that made Methodism what it was. But what kind of language was it? It was functional language that did not begin to suggest the experience it occasioned. Quarterly meeting had become a great ecclesial drama, a collective enactment of the Methodist meaning of the gospel. For whom would the phrase 'quarterly meeting' convey what the tradition had meant by *church,* that is, the unity of humanity experienced in Christ? Like the vernacular, Wesley's organizational terms were not suited for theological construction. Nor were they apt for the new sacramental meanings and responsibilities soon to be claimed.

If the vernacular was too idiosyncratic and if Wesley's language was inadequate for what his movement produced, would it do to superimpose terms from the church of origins? In 1784 when they organized themselves as the Methodist *Episcopal* Church, Methodists thought so. So the terminology of episcopal government was, admittedly at Wesley's direction, applied to the Methodist movement. But though the Anglican language represented what Methodists aspired to, it did not really capture what many Methodists felt they had come to be. It only partially connected with the richly textured community, fraternity, and order of Methodism. For all its legitimacy in the larger world, it invited Methodists into self-misunderstanding. The episcopal terminology prompted them to make the dynamic static, to change tasks into privileges, to transform belonging into status, to make order hierarchy.[28]

As Asbury noted, "We were in great haste, and did much business in a little time."[29] Whether with more leisure Methodists could have then or shortly thereafter reworked any of the languages or some combination into adequacy it is hard to know. The bishops tried with their explanatory notes on the 1798 *Discipline*. Would more creative spirits have felt at liberty, even with conference mandate? It is doubtful. Wesley's watchfulness while he lived and his intemperate response to the retitling of superintendency made such reworking highly impolitic. So the Americans took the prudent path and threw the languages together. Or perhaps it would be more accurate to say, they put the Wesleyan and Episcopal languages together in their *Discipline* and they seasoned their speech with a third, the vernacular.

The consequences of the misfit of language and Methodism were many, diverse, and long-term. Here we can only hint at them.

Implications

First, the linguistic cacophony yielded miscommunication. The languages awkwardly combined in the *Discipline* and the vernacular left out of it seem to have functioned as a coherent meaning system. However, Methodists did not work these several languages into explicit and formal coherence. Consequently, early Methodism had difficulty in transmitting its values to later generations. Successive conferences, to be sure, eventually rethought and reordered the *Discipline* so that the Anglican and Wesleyan idioms adhered. So privileged, that combination of tongues came to stand for Methodism. To that Methodists would appeal when faced with change and growth, when an appeal to legislative intentions was in order, when questions arose as to what Methodists had originally taught and been, when partisans debated the essence of Methodism. The dynamism of the vernacular, its place in the Methodist system of values and belief, and the ways it modified and enhanced the Anglican and Wesleyan idioms were easily lost.

Second, linguistic confusion bred conservatism. This is, indeed, ironic. One might think that linguistic imprecision would have prompted efforts at translation. As we have hinted above, some of the early divisions in Methodism reflected efforts to do just that. And yet they succeeded only partially. Perhaps it was Methodist pragmatism. The *Discipline* worked; its several languages worked. Perhaps it was loyalty to Wesley. He had given Methodism these languages. Surely they could employ them. Perhaps it was a Methodist sense of inferiority. American Methodists depended on Britain well into the nineteenth century, long after Mr. Wesley's shadow had faded. Perhaps to undertake terminological revision on central issues threatened the movement. In 1808, the General Conference adopted Restrictive Rules which guarded Articles of Religion and doctrine against revocation, alteration or change and put similar protections over government and rules. By those the church effectively blocked alteration and hence redefinition of its basic features. The formulations were perhaps not adequate but clarification itself endangered the genius of Methodism. Better to conserve than to translate.

Third, linguistic imprecision prompted apotheosis. Knowing that terms pointed to vital, essential facets of their movement, Methodists sanctified those terms. Words like 'conference', itinerancy', 'Discipline' acquired sacrality, and that act of sacralizing served eventually to mask their deeper meaning. It did so because the terms were insufficiently defined, because they did not, in fact, carry the resonances that made them worthy of sacralization, because their vernacular meaning was not indicated. Here, too, Methodist imprecision produced irony. Sacrality eventually attached itself to the form, to the surface, to the structure—not to the religious life originally borne by those externalities.

Miscommunication, conservatism, and apotheosis are perhaps most acutely internal Methodist problems. They are, however, also important problems for the interpreter. This chapter addresses the interpretative problems by rather deliberately coining and/or claiming new categories for analysis. Other chapters will take somewhat different tacks on the same set of problems. Here we have spoken of *community* in place of the more conventional terms revivalism and conversion, of *fraternity* instead of the more typical itinerancy and conference, of *order* in lieu of episcopacy and discipline.

The interpretive gain from this strategy can be illustrated with revivalism and conversion. Virtually all interpreters recognize early Methodist preoccupation with conversion, piety, perfection, and revivals. They also construe such religiosity as thoroughly individualistic, perhaps sharpening that judgment with the contrasting Methodist commitment to antislavery. The latter is taken to be exceptional or distinguished from other expressions of Methodist piety or indicative of what a more socially concerned piety would look like.

The truth is that antislavery was but one aspect of a communal reordering of the world. Both layperson and minister experienced early Methodism as profoundly social, collective, corporate, as we have shown. The Methodist categories initially conveyed, indeed mandated, that communal existence. Both the individual conversion and the aggregative revivalism were important for what they brought into being the Methodists, the new life together in Christ. Antislavery expressed the radical character Methodists perceived in that new community. It was, however, but one expression of that community.

In Methodism, as in evangelicalism generally, conversion and revivalism were so constitutive of Christian community that they were easily seen to be the essence of Christianity. When that happened, when revivalism became an end in itself, an interiorization and individualization of religion resulted. Then revivalism resembled its twentieth-century image and threatened to consume the community/communities that it had bred. This absolutizing of revivalism was an early nineteenth-century development. It occurred, as we shall see, as Methodism found its place in American society. The symbols of this change were many. One certainly was the retreat from antislavery. However, other dimensions of Methodist communal existence—other expressions of its profoundly communal character— were equally damaged by the absolutizing and ritualizing of revivals.

Revivalism and conversion never entirely lost their necessary connection with community, but they did become more individualistic. To many today they bear only individualistic meaning. To portray early Methodism revivalism as a communal affair, as we have in this chapter, is one way of overcoming the misimpressions created by current usage.

Itinerancy and conference have symbolized the Methodist fraternity of the word. As much as revivalism, they have suffered distortion from misemphasis, conservatism, and sacralization. These terms, too, became so familiar, so much a part of the day-to-day life of the movement, so constitutive of its structure that they seemed to require little definition. Their functions indicated meaning; their centrality indicated value; they acquired virtual sacrality. Definition and redefinition proved unnecessary. Over the years, drastic changes in American culture and religion— changes which radically reshaped Methodism—wrought dramatic alterations of itinerancy and conference. By the twentieth-century both had professional and organizational significance. These developments and the connotations they typically add to the rubrics cloud both the interpreter's and the insider's ability to understand early Methodism's itinerancy and conference. Terms like 'brotherhood' and 'brother' now come heavily laden with professional implications.

To be sure, recent studies have emphasized the covenantal character of the itinerancy.[30] Yet the full force of early Methodist fraternity is scarcely indicated. What was the source of its strength and character? It lay in the marriage-like bonds, the yoking in common responsibility, the intense working together, the sacrifices and risks that the preachers endured. This hazing had its purpose. Fraternity (and conference) deployed the ministry as a collective resource for the people called Methodists, as a collegium that assumed the plurality of ministerial tasks, as a (male) order in covenant to fulfill an evangelical mandate. Eventually these dimensions of early Methodism also succumbed to the individualizing lures of American society. For later periods it is appropriate to focus less on the fraternity and more on the individual tasks, prerogatives, and obligations of the ministerial office. For Methodists as for other Protestants, ministry would in the twentieth century become a profession.[31]

Fraternity not only directs interpretive attention from the individual to the collective. It also suggests, for early Methodism, that purpose rather than status and function took primary place in the life of the ministry and of the church. The fraternity pledged itself to ideals, to commitments, to the rigors of itinerancy that quite literally wore out the preachers. Worn-out preachers became a term of art for the movement, the result of high purposes triumphing over human energies. This was a purposive order, a preaching order.

To be sure, it was also a male order. It drew clear boundaries around itself. It excluded from its ranks persons whom later analysts might well think should have belonged. Both African Americans and women were excluded, though both, in fact, played vital and even preaching roles in the life of Methodism. Some interpreters might wish to shy away from a term like 'fraternity' in deference to today's expectations about inclusivity. Here we have retained 'fraternity', for to abandon it seems a mistake. The boundaries represented by the term were very important. Yet note, preachers called one another 'brother' in recognition of the familial bonds of love within which they labored. The commitments were of such depth that other loyalties did, indeed, threaten. But it was commitment to Christ and to one another that mattered. The hedges around that commitment—celibacy, whiteness, maleness, mobility—only reinforced the primary commitment.

Miscommunication, conservatism, and apotheosis manifestly affected order and discipline as well. Order was needed but was it necessary that episcopal authority be apotheosized in the way that it was? Clearly a substantial portion of the fraternity thought not. Early schisms point to the seriousness accorded this issue. Because episcopacy remained so central, so controversial, and so much under discussion, Methodists gave it more definitional precision than other categories we have examined. It is less problematic as an interpretive tool, though even here too its later meanings sometimes cloud its earliest manifestation. Discipline also is less disturbed by linguistic shifts than community and fraternity. Methodists preserved the earliest meanings of discipline by distinguishing the activity of discipline from their constitutional rendition of that order, the *Discipline*. Yet, over time the constitutional and political force of the latter tended to erode the full connotations of early Methodist discipline.

So interpreters turn into constitutional questions what for early Methodists were clearly also spiritual, eschatological, and ecclesial matters.

Finally, two points about the three values in relation to one another. Properly, Methodists held community, fraternity, and order in tension. But the tension was difficult to sustain. The clash of these values had much to do with the disharmonies of early Methodism. However, here as in the case of the values singly, the want of an adequate terminology made it difficult for the participants to conceive and think about the tension in these values and makes later attempts at interpretation and fidelity also difficult. For since Methodists did not formally identify these as concomitant values, since they accorded them no creedal significance, since they omitted them from *The Discipline*, they lacked banners with which to sustain the balance between community, fraternity, and order. And when they sought to conserve all three or when they fought out of differing commitment to one or two, they did so under less expressive standards. Not surprisingly, when we look back on their squabbles, we miss the issues that drove them. We are struck, instead, by the factors of power, personality, caste, or region. Those were certainly at play. But so too were these powerful ideals. History must recognize their role as well. The past will look somewhat different, for disputes in which only one side has been granted fidelity to Methodist standards will turn out to be struggles between values and fidelities.

Second, as we have shown, the community that Methodism offered the world was most complete when most public—in the quarterly meetings. There community, fraternity, and order balanced. And in the eighteenth century when Methodism was most complete, revival occurred. The point, by now obvious we hope, is that organization and life were one. This completeness, this unity of organization and life, was not indicated in the place where Methodism formally stated what it meant to be the church, namely in Article XIII of the *Articles of Religion*. That definition lacked the connectional and dynamic character of the quarterly meeting, providing instead a very conventional, congregational, Reformation conception. Such a definition also lacked the capacity to stipulate what had been another aspect of the quarterly meeting's ecclesial function, namely inclusivity. The quarterly meeting brought together Black and white, all classes, young and old, converted and unconverted. As Methodism came more to look like the church of the *Articles*, it lost much of this inclusivity. When Methodism boasted numbers adequate for a proper building and a stationed (rather than itinerating) preacher, it was difficult to keep Black and white, rich and poor together. Local churches, Methodists discovered, instinctively honor—not the quarterly meeting's penchant for inclusivity—but the world's rules of kinship, like with like. Methodism's own rules for classes (the unit within the church or society) honored such local custom. As Methodism congregationalized itself, it segregated. That process met no resistance or ethical pressure from the church's very congregational ecclesiological principle.

Methodism's exemplification of its ideal of the church was better than its theory. When Methodists gathered those who covenanted together to transcend the world's notions of kinship, they addressed one another as brother and sister, though of different neighborhood, family, class, and race—then they shouted. Methodists did not have a proper ecclesiological word for the quarterly meeting, a word to say that the church was the church when it met the world and offered itself as sacrament of the unity possible in Christ. But as we shall see in the next chapter, when they recognized themselves in the camp meeting of the early nineteenth century, they readily embraced the camp meeting. The camp meeting was no more ecclesiologically acceptable than quarterly meeting or 'melting' or 'sweet Christian conference' or 'stationing without trouble'. Early Methodism knew what it was about; it found no difficulty in proclaiming that from the stumps; it experienced great difficulty in expressing it in formal terms. Community, fraternity, and order may not say it completely. But perhaps it is a start.

2. From Quarterly to Camp Meeting

In a letter to Ezekiel Cooper dated 1795, Bishop Thomas Coke evoked various pleasures of America, including "the congregations in your forests."[1] A journal entry of four years earlier recalled:

> At each of our Conferences, before we parted every Preacher gave an account of his experience from the first strivings of the Spirit of God, as far as he could remember: and also of his call to preach, and the success the Lord had given to his labours. It was quite new, but was made a blessing I am persuaded to us all.[2]

What struck the British Dr. Coke as novelty—congregating in the woods and the spiritually communal and revivalistic character of conferences—were but two images of early American Methodist vitality. Their conjunction some time later in the camp meeting[3] provided Methodism with a metaphor of itself. The camp meeting, as a self-image, as an intricate and highly stylized recapitulation of the American Methodist experience, allowed Methodism to change while seeming to remain the same.[4]

The camp meeting was at once something new and yet continuous with earlier American Methodism. Sufficiently a novelty to require promotion, it quickly spread over Methodism to become a national institution. Frontier weapon perhaps it was. But some of the camp meeting's power to create frontier community derived from its ritual reenactment of earlier Methodist community. It was a new way of reliving the old and an old way for living in the new.

The "Frontier" Camp Meeting

To place the camp meeting in the economy of Methodism is to deny that it was exclusively a frontier affair. Ironically, those most responsible for

21

so imprinting it did so by allowing the rubrics and limits of their studies to overwhelm their evidence and commentary. The statement in Charles A. Johnson's title, *The Frontier Camp Meeting*, probably is the major culprit. When endorsed and appropriated by his mentor, the then-dean of American church historians, William Warren Sweet, and worked into his frontier reading of American religion,[5] "the frontier camp meeting" became a historical commonplace.[6]

Johnson clearly conceives the camp meeting as a frontier affair. A "weapon . . . forged by the West in its struggle against lawlessness and immorality," a "natural product of a frontier environment," a religious expression suited to the frontier mentality, the camp meeting evolved "with the prevailing intellectual climate" of the region. As the frontier disappeared so also did the camp meeting.[7] These judgments prevail. Yet lurking throughout Johnson's interpretation are the qualifications that would sabotage it. He concedes that it had eastern antecedents; that after its adoption by Asbury, the camp meeting was promoted in the East; that promotion, population density, and receptivity governed frequency and size; that camp meetings became popular in areas that were not frontiers demographically or frontiers for Methodism.[8] Johnson contents himself with such qualifications because it is not his purpose to treat either American Protestantism or Methodism on a national basis. "The scope of the book," he indicates, "is limited to the trans-Allegheny West in the first four decades of the nineteenth century."[9]

This protective delimitation and qualification, however, fails to counterbalance the forceful assertion: "The camp meeting fires previously lighted in Kentucky continued to burn brightly in section after section of the new nation as the traveling ministry followed migrants toward other frontiers."[10] The energy of his images stamped the camp meeting as a frontier affair. That, we shall suggest, misconstrues its orientation and function.

The "Methodist" Camp Meeting

To place the camp meeting in the economy of Methodism is to remove it, rather arbitrarily, from its premier place in "the great revival," from its continuing role as a largely Methodist undertaking in nineteenth-century revivalistic procedures that were largely shared, and from its part in the production of an evangelical ethos which functioned as the vehicle for the national establishment of Christianity, points about the camp meeting effectively made by John B. Boles,[11] Dickson D. Bruce, Jr.,[12] and Donald G. Mathews.[13]

The value of these larger perspectives is so obvious that the resort to a denominational view may seem a scholarly retreat. This estimate of the camp meeting in Methodist perspective will prove quite complementary. It addresses the question why Methodism found the camp meeting congenial. Not at issue is authorship. This attention to the continuities between the camp meeting and prior Methodist experience is not intended as a restatement of Methodist claims of creation. Nor would it jeopardize that attempt to link the camp meeting with prior religious experience in other denominations. And it certainly is not intended to obscure that fact that in its first several years the camp meeting was a catholic endeavor, joining the creative energies of Presbyterians, Baptists, and Methodists. The claims of James McGready, the Presbyterians, and the state of Kentucky are not challenged. Rather we pursue possible historical grounds for this 1802 episcopal directive:

> The campmeetings have been blessed in North and South Carolina, and Georgia. Hundreds have fallen and have felt the power of God. I wish most sincerely that we could have a campmeeting at Duck Creek out in the plain south of the town, and let the people come with their tents, wagons, provisions and so on. Let them keep at it night and day, during the conference; that ought to sit in the meeting.[14]

What prompted Asbury's design to put conference and camp meeting together, and to do so not in the wilderness but in Methodism's citadel, Baltimore? Was there more than pragmatism in Asbury's adoption of this "fishing with a large net?"[15] What might have predisposed Methodist preachers and people to structure their community in sylvan settings? Why did Methodism adopt the camp meeting?[16]

Reenactment

The camp meeting was a ritual recovery of unities, openness, inclusiveness, and flexibility that had characterized early American Methodism. It appeared and found favor at that point sociologists label with phrases like "the ritualization of charisma" or "the dilemmas of institutionalization,"[17] the point where the world's lines are drawn, prerogatives appear, racial, economic, and sexual differentiation is marked, and rules triumph. The camp meeting vividly reenacted the early preacher's encounter with the American landscape (an encounter that to be sure continued). In its action it recalled the memory of intense community and the dramatic revivalistic response at Methodist conferences—quarterly and annual. Yet by its staging, locale, and purpose—even when combined with quarterly and annual conferences—the camp meeting permitted conferences to occupy themselves with the business of the denomination. Encampments could not be an official Methodist institution for that would have forced Methodists to recognize the profound changes that numerical growth, time, distance, diversity, and aging produced. Instead it was a historical drama, a play that Methodists performed for themselves and the world, a staging of their own history by which they drew upon and shared what had created them. Methodists were too preoccupied with the Holy Spirit to recognize the dilemmas of institutionalization. They had discovered what for a time seemed to be a device for circumventing them. The camp meeting allowed Methodism to change while seeming to remain the same.

What Methodism in the early nineteenth century would reenact was well described in 1810 by Jesse Lee. Speaking of 1776, he wrote:

> On Tuesday and Wednesday, the 30th and 31st day of July, quarterly-meeting was held at Mabury's dwelling house in *Brunswick* (now Greenville) county. No meeting-house in *Virginia* could have held the people. We had a large arbour in the yard, which would shade from the sun, two or three thousand people. The first day was a blessed season; but the second day was a day never to be forgotten. We held the love-feast under the arbour in the open air; the members of society took their seats, and other people stood all around them by hundreds. The place was truly awful, by reason of the presence of the Lord. Many of the members spake; and while some declared how the Lord had justified them freely, others declared how, and when the blood of Jesus had cleansed them from all sin. So clear, so full, and so strong was their testimony, that while some were speaking their experience, hundreds were in tears, and others vehemently crying to God, for pardon or holiness.
>
> Such a work of God as that was, I had never seen, or heard of before. It continued to spread through the south parts of *Virginia*, and the adjacent parts of *North-Carolina*, all that summer and autumn.[18]

For all the novelty of camping, the stylizing of time by rules and of space by camp design and the prolongation of meeting itself, the camp meeting was highly evocative of patterns with which Methodists were very familiar. For the preachers especially, they called to mind what Lee described, the communal gatherings that had symbolized a new order of existence.

Conference as Revival

The Minutes for 1780 query: "Shall we recommend our quarterly meetings to be held on Saturdays and Sundays when convenient?" and answer:

"Agreed."[19] This legislation regularized what was apparently already practiced and placed them so as to make them popularly accessible.[20] The two-day events had acquired a definite pattern but one that permitted variation. The first day was devoted to the business of the circuit, finances, discipline, and to some preaching. On the second day, love feast began at 9:00, followed perhaps by communion around 11:00, then "public preaching" at noon. Memorial services, marriages, baptisms might be interspersed or follow.[21] Three communities gathered. The one most remarked upon was the general populace. Of a 1780 meeting at Thomas Chapel, Delaware, Freeborn Garrettson noted: "Blest be God it appeared as if the whole country came together." He reiterated those words for a quarterly meeting at Bolingbroke. At others that year he estimated crowds of 2,000, 1,500, and "near 4,000."[22]

Particularly for the areas of Methodist strength—Delaware, Maryland, Virginia—the significance of such gatherings cannot be stressed too much. In these gentry-dominated societies, laced together by waterways and largely wanting the towns that provided communal coherence in New England, community quite literally occurred. As we have already seen, the social order defined itself by act rather than space. Ceremonies that exhibited and reinforced the values and preoccupations of the gentry ritualized community. Court days, quarter races, cock fights, dances, musters, elections, and Anglican services occasioned social interaction. The established religion of the society, it has been suggested, was patriarchy; it demanded deference rather than prayers, and it took the Church of England as servant.

The evangelicalism of Presbyterians, then Baptists, and finally Methodists that penetrated this patriarchal world in the second half of the eighteenth century perforce offered counter-creed, counter-culture, and counter-community.[23] The quarterly meeting served the Methodists quite well in this regard. In a society which dramatized and actualized the community of honor and deference, quarterly meeting provided a striking alternative. The quarterly meeting staged, as it were, the free grace that Methodists preached. It must have seemed that Christian community quite literally offered itself in public. After ordering and nourishing themselves, those Methodists who seemingly loved one another opened their community to the public. Freeborn Garrettson caught the drama. After "a crowded audience" on August 5, 1781, Sunday began at 9:00 in "a comfortable feast of love." Then from 12 to 4 "many happy souls feasted with us."[24] As Garrettson and his compatriots described it, the quarterly meeting was a public ceremony, like those familiar to and a basis of community in Chesapeake society. However, it countered those hierarchical-deferential gentry expressions of patriarchal community with an inclusive and spiritually egalitarian alternative. Further, the public first witnessed and then was invited to join that new community. A 1792 quarterly meeting reported by Cooper captures this embracive quality:

> Saturday, February 18, 1792. We went on to quarterly meeting. The house was crowded. We had a tolerable time.
>
> Sunday, 19. In love-feast the Lord was precious, but in the time of preaching he opened the windows of heaven and poured down blessings upon us. Sinners were struck as with hammer and fire, or like as if thunder flashes had smitten them. A general cry began, so that I was forced to stop preaching. I stood upon the stand and looked on, and saw them in every part of the congregation with streaming eyes, and groaning for mercy, while others were shouting praises to God for delivering grace. Numbers were converted—the season was truly glorious and very refreshing to God's dear people. The meeting never broke up till about sundown.[25]

'Opened windows' aptly captured Methodism's sense of its gospel and itself. In the quarterly meeting, Methodism dramatically opened its community, opened its windows, to attest the sincerity and dependability of the grace promised and so freely assured. This event was then a public event, gathering in all from the larger community who would come.

Two other communities also met. The second community gathered in the quarterly meeting was that of the Methodist circuit. Both before 1784 and for a long time thereafter for many circuits, the quarterly meeting was the point at which members experienced the full dimensions of Methodist community. Before 1784 when its itinerants were not ordained and were (with some notable exceptions) not celebrating the Eucharist, the love feast with its intense sharing of Christian experience must have been the liturgical heart of the two days. After 1784, love feast and Lord's supper must have vied in some fashion for liturgical primacy.[26] At any rate, the quarterly meeting was the event in the calendar of Methodism when these expressions of the whole church were made available. The quarterly meeting also brought face-to-face those knit by administrative duties, financial obligations, and leadership. It was the time when the people who shared itinerants, local preachers, exhorters were together. They had a certain amount of business to do and certain duties that could only be done legally when gathered quarterly.[27]

But the two days surrounded those administrative tasks with the full range of Methodist religious experiences. The faithful needed no book of services; quarterly meeting dramatized them. Even the class meeting, which was not replicated, was in a sense represented since its acts of inclusion or exclusion pointed toward the events of quarterly meeting. The quarterly meeting was, then, the occasion when the Methodists who belonged together were gathered, with all their leaders, to enjoy the feast of Methodist religious offerings and to perform those offices it made incumbent on itself as church. For all these reasons but particularly the latter, at the quarterly meeting Methodism became, in its own terms though as we have seen not in its theory, a church. In these strange occasions Methodism was most distinctively itself.

The distinctiveness of the occasion had much to do with the third community gathered by the quarterly meeting. The quarterly meeting brought the ministry together. Asbury noted of one in 1781, "We had twelve preachers, and about one thousand people at quarterly meeting."[28] While by no means as large or regionally inclusive as the annual conference, the quarterly meeting partook of its fraternal character. Cooper, more discerning and attentive to detail than many of his compatriots, reported of a Kent Circuit, Delaware quarterly meeting of 1785 that after love feast at 9:00: "Then preaching, in and out of doors, began at twelve o'clock. Brother Whatcoat preached within, Brother Cloud outside. George Moore gave an exhortation in, and Harry, a black man, exhorted without. It was a good time.[29] As Cooper's statement indicates, the quarterly meeting could be far more inclusive than more local Methodist gatherings—the class and society—where segregation had already appeared. The quarterly meeting was more racially inclusive than local or regional affairs, in part, because it embraced every level of Methodist leadership: bishop, presiding elder, elder, deacon, local preacher, exhorter, class leader, steward. Inclusiveness was part of its purpose. To be sure, it must have been unusual to have the numbers of traveling preachers that Asbury occasionally records, "a dozen preachers besides others,"[30] he noted in 1786. But the fact is that when conference—quarterly, annual, or later general—was the destination, Methodists often traveled in entourage. (It might be noted, incidentally, that the traveling together might have mitigated both the exercise and the perception of Methodist authority, making the movement seem more egalitarian than it actually was.) At any rate, on the way to quarterly meeting, the bishop or presiding elder would gather in traveling and local preachers, exhorters, and class leaders and meet others at the destination.[31] All would be active at the resulting gathering.

Their gathering had a very special, spiritual intensity. Garrettson caught this dimension when he affirmed of a 1777 gathering: "I was greatly refreshed among the servants of God."[32] The Preachers experienced that renewal on the various occasions when they were together. James Meacham proclaimed, "Sweet is the Company of the preachers."

He frequently employed the phrase "sweet Christian Conference" to register the depth of interpersonal engagement among Methodists. "We had Sweet conferences together," he affirmed after meeting with an individual, with a family, with several ministers, and especially in quarterly conference.[33]

At quarterly meeting, then, Methodist people and the public witnessed the deep engagement of ministers with ministers. The drama that unfolded derived some of its intensity from the heightened sensitivity and mutual stimulation of the ministers. Their proclamation and praise had the strength of numbers, the intensity a support group provides, and the creative nurture afforded by peer review. At quarterly meeting the collegium performed.

Methodists struggled for adequate language to convey what occurred. Asbury noted for a 1779 quarterly meeting:

> Our love feast began at nine, and public worship at twelve o'clock. The operations of the Holy Spirit were very powerful in the congregation; so that there was a general melting; and amongst the young people, there were outcries and deep distress. Here was a blessed prospect, God is gracious beyond the power of language to describe. Both preachers and people were exceedingly quickened. The public labours of the day were too much for my feeble frame.[34]

For early Methodists what captured the meaning of the quarterly meeting, what improved on rhetoric's most extravagant claims, was revival. Revival attested, in their world, what words could not. Revival said, of course, that the event was of God. When revivals followed quarterly meetings in July and August of 1789, Garrettson noted in his journal: a "great meeting, perhaps the greatest that we have ever known in this side of the North River."[35] For Garrettson and early Methodism, those superlatives pointed to the pouring out of the Holy spirit, to the providential character of Methodism, to its redemptive purposes.

Methodists had no difficulty in specifying those dimensions of the quarterly meeting, either by assertion or description. Their claims (as claims) need to be honored today in scholarly analyses even if we would not reiterate them in early Methodism's terms. And we need to elaborate the premises that made the providential conclusions come so easily. Charles Grandison Finney would do that later by detailing "When a Revival is to be Expected," and then itemizing those factors that promote or hinder its production.[36] Early Methodists lacked Finney's confidence that the Spirit could be so manipulated. They did have some clarity about those aspects of their own life that, in their view, served faithfully to permit the giving of the Spirit. We have rendered those premised or Methodists aspects as: the full and open display of Methodist offices; in a public arena; to a gathering of all those who comprised the Methodist community as well as all from the larger community who would come; during a period both extended enough to permit the several rituals and yet accessible to those with leisure and those who worked, those with freedom and those without, those who tended children and those who did not—Saturday and Sunday serving this function well; with the clear indication by word (the universality of grace) and dramatization by act (the public preaching) of Methodism's inclusivity; to the end that a disciplined and holy life be offered to individuals and community. In the quarterly meeting, Methodism dramatized itself as a gracious vessel. Revival, in their view, fittingly applauded.

For early Methodist the true test of Christian fellowship was the pouring out of the Holy Spirit. Revival following quarterly meeting proclaimed that when Methodists were knit in common purpose and deeply felt unity, their community was the message. The quarterly meeting revival was Methodism being blessed in consequence of being itself. Organization and revival, inner life and public testimony cohered.

At times the annual conferences and later even General Conferences had such a revivalistic thrust. Of the General Conference of 1800 it is reported: "[A] great revival began during the Conference and perhaps near 50 were converted mostly young persons . . . Conference broke up on the 20th . . . More than 100 Souls were awakened & converted & the revival Continues."[37] Annual conferences possessed and continued to possess that potential. Lee ascribed 1788 revivals in Maryland, both eastern and western shores, to conference preaching. Asbury credited one of the conferences in 1789 and one in 1790 with that result.[38] Although annual conferences (and general conferences) were highly important in the furthering of ministerial fraternity, their potential as agencies of conversion was minimized by both their closed nature and the burden of issues, conflict, and business they increasingly bore. The judgments that Asbury levied, "peace and love," "peace and union," "peace and order,"[39] projected a fraternal ideal. The ideal contended with the reality that the conference (annual and general) served also as legislature, administration, judiciary. Furthermore, the conference struggled to understand its functions while tugged simultaneously by the republican ideals of American society and the spiritually concentrated patterns exercised by Wesley and inherited by Asbury, points elaborated elsewhere in this volume. Here it is only important to observe that in the annual conference as in the quarterly—in early Methodism—spirituality and business lay side by side. Indeed to shift the image, they could be the two sides of one coin. Hearing the testimony of the persons at the various stages of candidacy—the consuming task of annual conference—was administration that could be inspiring, instructive, renewing, and certainly community-building.

But as Methodism prospered, as numbers of circuits, preachers and members increased, as the number of conferences grew dramatically—from one in 1781 to fourteen by the end of the decade—and as divisive issues preoccupied the attendees, the spirituality of conference suffered. The business of the church required new legislation; various crises made conference inevitably more and more an administrative, even a political arena.

Then, great wonder of wonders, a miracle. Methodism discovered how to have its cake and eat it too. Methodism discovered how to change while remaining unchanged. Methodism discovered how to have conference as business without sacrificing conference as revival. Methodism discovered the camp meeting. Or perhaps better, the camp meeting discovered Methodism. For the camp meeting was a miraculous mirror, a wonderful looking glass that allowed Methodism to see itself just as it wanted to be. The camp meeting was Methodism all in spirit, Methodist means serving Methodist ends, conference as revival. Yet it could not be formally incorporated into the Methodist *Discipline.* That would shatter the illusion.

Revival: From Quarterly to Camp Meeting

There are three rather remarkable contemporaneous literary documentations of Methodism's discovery of itself in the camp meeting. All three have some claim to an official stamp. The first to appear were accounts in *The Methodist Magazine* (London), which in the absence of an American Methodist publication carried some American religious intelligence. These seem to have an official American anchor at one or both ends. Bishop Coke was the recipient of some of the correspondence. Ezekiel Cooper, superintendent of Methodism's publishing and marketing efforts, the Book Concern, wrote some and may well have sent others.[40] The second item to appear was a volume entitled *Extracts of Letters Containing some Account of the Work of God Since the Year 1800. Written by the Preachers and Members of the Methodist Episcopal Church, to their Bishops*[41] which appeared in 1805, also, it might be noted, under Cooper's agency. The third was Lee's *Short-History* finished in 1809 but published in 1810.

Lee had a longer view than the other two but all three had revival as their basic motif. And in all three revival is borne first by the quarterly meeting and then by the camp meeting. In the period leading up to 1801, when he recognized the first camp meeting, Lee accounted all Methodist growth as revival. His own successes in gathering Methodists out of Congregationalist New England have that designation. Lee gave special attention to five revivals. In three of these, the quarterly conference is the dramatic center; in the other two annual or general conference.[42] After 1801, Lee associated revival with camp meetings or camp meetings held as quarterly meetings.[43] Lee, then, construed revival as initially a matter of conference and then a matter of camp meeting. Camp meetings succeeded conference as the foundation of revival. The transition is subtle but, in Lee, one can follow Methodism's discovery of itself in the camp meeting.

The letters in both *The Methodist Magazine* and *Extracts* are themselves a barometer of the revival. Asbury wrote Coke in August 1801 that revivals among Methodists and Presbyterians had occurred in Tennessee but also on "every Circuit upon the Eastern and Western Shores"; there is even "a stir in Jersey."[44] Another correspondent informed an English Methodist of "the revival of Religion in America." "It is said there never was such an out-pouring of the Spirit, as there is at present thro' most parts of the Continent." After reporting first hand on the revivals in the Baltimore circuit, he detailed the Kentucky and Tennessee Presbyterian-Methodist encampments, relying on and citing correspondence from there.[45] In the letters that follow attention is on the camp meetings, doubtless intriguing to the largely English readership, but quarterly meetings and great meetings are also featured.[46] It is difficult to read through these letters without sensing, first, that the camp meetings were experienced as a novelty, but second, that they were immediately adopted as an expansion in time and scale of the quarterly meeting. The same conclusion is to be drawn from the *Extracts* which report quarterly meetings, annual meetings, and many camp meetings.[47] Here the chronological arrangement of the letters permits the reader to look over Methodist shoulders as the camp meeting is recognized as something congenial. This volume is Methodism, in official capacity, reporting itself in transition.

The role of Asbury in the appropriation of the camp meeting cannot be minimized. He saw immediately that camp meetings worked for Methodism. However, the task was made easy because Methodism as a whole recognized itself in the camp meeting. The letters made that very clear. Cooper, who had experienced the following (pre–camp meeting) Dover annual meeting, would understandably have little difficulty in embracing the later camp meeting as familiar and congenial. The differences consisted only in tents.

The week previous to the Conference there was a great meeting at Dover. It began on Whitsunday, and continued a whole week. It was a glorious time indeed. I was there four or five days. Thousands attended; people came near a hundred miles to that meeting, and many were there from thirty, forty and fifty miles distant. Our preaching house could not hold much more than a tenth of them. and surely it was a pentecost indeed! On whitsunday I preached . . . I stood in a waggon, and was surrounded by thousands of attentive souls. . . . [48]

Thomas Ware, looking back from the vantage of the 1840s on the same phenomenon, the Dover annual meeting and its consequent revival, recognized the same affinity between quarterly and camp meeting: "Camp meetings had not yet been introduced; and we knew not what to do with the thousands who attended our quarterly meetings. sometimes we were forced to resort to the woods, and even to hold our love-feasts in the grove."[49]

Conclusions

The testimony of Cooper and Ware point to the following conclusions: (1) The most important factor in the emergence of the camp meetings as a national, quasi-official institution was their essential continuity with quarterly meeting and annual conference, especially the former. (2) That continuity calls attention to an insufficiently stressed characteristic of early Methodist revivals. They were seated in conference, in quarterly meeting and annual conference especially. (3) That unity of revival and machinery, of evangelism and organization, of life and order proved difficult to sustain as Methodism grew in numbers, area, complexity. (4) The camp meeting caught on as a revitalization measure which mirrored or replicated early patterns (i.e., the quarterly meeting). (5) Its ability to safeguard Methodist ethos permitted the evolution of order into organization, of conference into business, of *Discipline* into constitution to proceed. In short, the camp meeting allowed Methodism to change while appearing to remain the same.

3. Views of the Nation
A Glass to the Heart

All the prospects of this world are dead to
me. I feel not a wish for creatures or things.
The glory of the Kingdom of Christ, the
organization of a primitive Church of God,
these are all my objects; was it possible to set
a glass to my heart, you should see them
engraven there by the word & spirit of the
living God.[1]

Francis Asbury's image encapsulates this chapter's argument. Early American Methodists, strictly speaking, lacked a concept of the nation. Of its existence they were painfully aware! Wartime persecutions and imprisonments, loss of leadership and membership to Britain and Canada, trying efforts to indigenize authority made them acutely conscious that they lived in a new nation. Yet, they simply looked right through the nation. They did not see it. They had, as it were, a glass to its heart. When they gazed in its direction, they saw through it to dominions they deemed more important.

The point may seem obvious. However, some of the implications may be less so. Early Methodists, we know, drew a line between God's people and the children of the devil.[2] Their loyalty was to the power and polity erected on the heavenward side of that line. With temporal power they had ultimately little to do. Asbury lectured McKendree just so in his valedictory:

As to temporal power, what have we to do with that in this country? We are not senators, congressmen, or chaplains; neither do we hold any civil offices. We neither have, nor wish to have, anything to do with the government of the States, nor, as I conceive, do the States fear us. Our kingdom is not of this world. For near half a century we have never grasped at power.[3]

33

But these same apolitical Methodists struggled with themselves up to 1784 over how to achieve American legitimacy, in 1784 became the first denomination to organize themselves nationally, from that date were the most national American church, were staunchly 'American', prided themselves on their patriotism, were, in short, a typically 'American church' in the many meanings of that phrase.

Why the apparent paradox? How could Methodists be at once completely oblivious to and highly conscious of their American nationality? Why would they be so insistent on their indifference to the world and American society and so intent on establishing their American credentials? Why the aversion to politics and the passion for patriotism? Why the biformity, to use Michael Kammen's term,[4] of laboring to attain what was thought inconsequential?

Parallels do not really solve the problem. To be sure, similar apparently contradictory attitudes toward American society abound. One recent interpreter argues that such ambivalences actually characterize American religious movements.[5] They certainly typify sectarian movements, ethnic denominations, peace churches, and Roman Catholicism. With the first three of those Methodism shared characteristics to a limited extent and particularly during its first decade. Here, though, we treat Methodism in its next phrase—from 1784 through the second decade of the nineteenth century. Methodism was no longer an Irish movement, if it ever was, but rather multiethnic. Nor would pacifism or sectarianism characterize it then. (Some who have reflected seriously about the nature of sectarianism and denominationalism suggest that Methodism never underwent a sectarian phase.[6]) And the contrasts of patriotism and dissent or patriotism and alienation that characterized those three patterns and Roman Catholicism differed from that of Methodism. The Methodists did not simply want to be left alone by the nation. They wanted to convert it.

Nor can this puzzle be dismissed with the misguided twentieth-century commonplace that early evangelicalism was inherently individualistic and otherworldly and hence oblivious to the nation. We now have rather considerable evidence that many in the evangelical camp, particularly around its Reformed (Presbyterian/Congregational) fires, worked assiduously during this same period, after the Revolution and particularly after the Constitutional Convention, to reassociate, not dissociate, religion and nation. Fred J. Hood, who has analyzed these efforts, refers to hundreds of Reformed sermons which insisted on the "natural connection between religion and national prosperity."[7] Facing legal disestablishment and recognizing religious pluralism as a given, other evangelical Protestants began erecting the voluntary establishment of Christianity.

The Methodist pattern seems to cut against the grain. And note, we speak not of inconsequential variations in denominational preachments. Across important sectors of American society, the nature of the republic had become a religious affair, a sacred trust, and Americans invested the nation with terms heretofore reserved for the church.[8] In a society super-saturated with republican programs, concerns, theories, a society intent on properly conceiving the relation of religion and the nation, the Methodists remain uncharacteristically quiet and aloof. Why? Obviously, a partial answer has to do with the Revolutionary experience—that politics divided Methodists; that the Tory imprint could not be totally explained away; that leadership remained British. And yet the answer lies also elsewhere, within the heart.

"God's Design in Raising Up the Preachers Called Methodists"

Perhaps we had best begin at the end, at the point of critical transition, when the nation came more fully into Methodist consciousness. "Dearly Beloved Brethren," intoned William McKendree in the 1816 episcopal address, "We believe God's design in raising up the preachers called Methodists in America, was to reform the continent by spreading scriptural holiness over these lands."[9] So, we have been instructed, McKendree collapsed the two-fold purpose of Methodism—reform and spreading scriptural holiness—into one. The simple substitution of preposition for conjunction, of the word 'by' for the word 'and' had deeper significance. That substitution, it is sometimes argued, symbolized the broader reconception of Methodist purpose. It signaled the faltering of Methodist commitment to reform. Evangelism became the sole end of Methodist action and reform was given an evangelical content.[10]

The relation of reform to Methodist purpose is a matter to which we will return. At this juncture, it is important to extract from this episode the assumption undergirding such constructions, namely the recognition that the language of this statement of purpose is to be taken seriously. Early Methodists apparently thought so. The statement appeared as the answer to the fourth question in the *Discipline* of 1784: "What may we reasonably believe to be God's Design in raising up the Preachers called Methodists? A. To reform the Continent, and to spread scriptural Holiness over these lands." In 1787 when the *Discipline* was "Arranged under proper HEADS, and METHODIZED in a more acceptable and easy Manner," they added, "As a Proof hereof, we have seen in the Course of fifteen Years a great and glorious Work of God, from New York through the Jersies, Pennsylvania, Maryland, North and South Carolina, even to Georgia." In 1790 the purpose was transformed from question into affirmative statement and included in the prefatory episcopal address, "To the Members of the Methodist Societies in the United States."[11] There it remained until well after our period, to be endorsed by the names of the current bishops.

To Reform the Continent

If, then, this statement of purpose assumed critical importance for early Methodists, an earlier and perhaps more important alteration in it than the one executed by McKendree deserves attention. The change in question occurred in the transformation of the constitution of British Methodism, *The Large Minutes*, into the first *Discipline*.

Wesley's formulation had been, "To reform the Nation, particularly the Church; and to spread scriptural holiness over the Land." The Christmas Conference altered that to the familiar, "To reform the Continent, and to spread scriptural Holiness over these lands."[12] The Americans substituted "continent" for Wesley's "the Nation, particularly the Church." They also made the singular "Land" plural. In themselves, these changes might seem insignificant, a recognition that American Methodism labored in a religiously plural situation, not within the Church of England, and operated across rather than within what had been the important jurisdictional lines.[13] Yet, like McKendree's alteration, they symbolize larger patterns.

American Methodists, under Asbury's leadership, oriented themselves to America as continent rather than as nation; to its physical environment, its lands rather than its polity; to geography rather than civitas. This insight was initially stimulated not as here implied by reflection on this statement of purpose. That connection came later. Rather it derived from a reading of Asbury's journal. The purpose of that reading was to discern his conception of America and Americanization. What proved particularly arresting were recurrent references to America as continent, statements like the following: "You cannot, you dare not," Asbury wrote Coke in 1797, "but consider yourself as a servant of the church, and a citizen of the continent of America."[14] The notion that Methodist citizenship vested in the continent assumed the character of a formula. For the Baltimore conference of 1802, Asbury recorded, "We had a day of fasting and humiliation for the conference, the continent, and the Church of God. . . . " A month later for the Philadelphia conference, Asbury spoke of "a day of fasting and prayer to be observed on the fourth of May, for the conference, the Church in general, and the continent at large." In New

York in June, he noted, "We had a day of solemn fasting and prayer for the Church, the conference, the continent, and for the world. . . . "[15]

In part, citizenship in continent and nation said what page after page of Asbury's journal and that of his fellow itinerants also said. America presented itself to Methodists as forests, rivers, roads, clearings, mountains, swamps. Their journals can be read as sustained meditations upon the physical character of America. Actually the available version of Asbury's journal disguises the continent's immediacy. His twentieth-century editors chose to put state names as page headings over Asbury's entries. By superimposing political boundaries on Asbury's itinerations, helpful as it may be to the conference historian, the editors actually mask the sheer enormity and physical salience of the land to Asbury. He and colleagues who traveled day after day, week after week, experienced America as geography and appropriately then conceived it in spatial rather than political terms. Yet the preference for continent rather than nation in the formulation of Methodist purpose derived from more than physical hardship on the land.

A Just and Lawful Submission to Their Rulers

Methodists focused upon America's physical nature rather than its social or political, upon America as continent rather than America as society or state, in part because they experienced the land so directly. That focus, however, had very much to do with their view of political society.

Prior to the Revolution, Methodists could, and for the most part did, simply ignore the state. The Revolution made the matter of allegiance critical for all in the colonies, the Methodists included. As a movement under the direct leadership of British preachers, shaped by and responsible to a Wesley who had spoken against the cause of independence, drawing constituents from the Church of England and in a few instances harboring active Tories, Methodists labored under suspicion and at times suffered persecution during the Revolution.[16] Methodist response to the Revolution and reaction to these suspicions ran the gamut. One or two of the leaders championed the Tory cause while remaining in the colonies; most of the British preachers returned home; a sizable portion of the Methodist folk moved then or thereafter to Canada; Asbury went into seclusion; a few, most notably Freeborn Garrettson, adopted a high profile pacifism; and many, including some who would be important ministers, as for instance Thomas Ware, served as chaplains or combatants on the revolutionary side.

Revolution, the new nation, and eventually the Constitution made a position vis-à-vis America imperative. Methodism could not continue to avoid civil authority in the fashion of Asbury during the Revolution. They did not. In a variety of ways, Methodism indicated its at-homeness in the new society. The most notable of such gestures was its own quest for independence, a process that began during the Revolution and culminated in the establishment of the Methodist Episcopal Church in 1784.

Methodism embraced American society in less demonstrative ways. Preachers' journals, for instance, show not a small amount of pride in the persons of position and means, of political power and of social standing, to whom access is gained. Such notes, for the record, imply a more positive or at least ambivalent relation to society and state than our first two citations from Asbury would suggest. Methodism did make its way into American society.

Yet, ambivalence did seem to be the order of the day. Though aware of itself as a newly independent movement in a newly independent nation, such a position did not elicit strikingly self-conscious reflection about the nation and Methodism's relation thereunto. And the exceptional instances of Methodist political utterance betray the ambiguity here under review, of being in but not of the nation.

For instance, Methodists prided themselves in the fact that their bishops were the first religious leaders to address President Washington. That address is sometimes cited as instancing Methodist views of the nation. Theodore Linn, for instance, argues that the delegation's language provided "the interpretive framework within which Methodists understood their task in relation to the new nation." He discerns in the text the following:

> First, the nation's successful revolt is attributed to God's providential activity in human history. Second, God, as moral governor of the universe, is the source of every blessing, but most particularly, the source of the constitution of the new nation. Third, the nation is perceived to be at the center of the world's attention. . . . Fourth . . . it may be the example for the world. . . . Fifth, it is expected that the government of the United States can be and will be both impartial and supportive of "genuine, vital religion." Finally, the religious community has the responsibility to support the government.[17]

Linn is most assuredly correct in his first point, that Methodists read history in providential terms. Both the fact and message of the address assured the new President of Methodist support, his sixth point. These statements, by themselves, would constitute a very weak civil theology.

On the important assertions, another construction can be put on the text than that adopted by Linn. The three vital affirmations of this civil theology can be read as characterizations of Washington, not Methodist affirmations. One other point, the exemplary force of the Constitution, is a kind of aside. The relevant portion of the address asserted:

> We have received the most grateful satisfaction, from the humble and entire dependence on the Great Governor of the universe which you have repeatedly expressed, acknowledging him the source of every blessing, and particularly of the most excellent constitution of these states, which is at present the admiration of the world, and may in future become its great exemplar for imitation: and hence we enjoy a holy expectation that you will always prove a faithful and impartial patron of genuine, vital religion—the grand end of our creation and present probationary existence. And we promise you our fervent prayers to the throne of grace, that GOD Almighty may endue you to fill up your important station to his glory, the good of his church, the happiness and prosperity of the United States, and the welfare of mankind.[18]

In the final sentence, Methodists assured Washington of their prayers. But in the long, image-rich first sentence they itemized Washington's belief, not their own. The address might be read as the highest form of tribute, the evocation of Washington's own affirmations, uttered only a month earlier in his First Inaugural.[19] Is it, then, an expression of Washington's civil theology, not the Methodists'?

Even grant Linn that such terms, in whatever mouth, constitute a civil theology, grant even further that Methodists by their composing them evidence awareness of such perceptions of civil authority, then all the more remarkable becomes the sparsity of Methodist commentary about the nation.

When Methodists did make proclamations about the nation, they did so in ambivalent terms, terms that could well be invoked for government anywhere. Early Methodists did not, as would their descendants in 1865 through their centenary objective, "consider the responsibility of Methodists to do their share in educating the conscience of the nation so as to make this a truly Christian nation."[20] Notions of America as God's chosen people, of a covenant between God and the nation, of eternal purposes being worked out through the American experiment, of America as the light to the world, of religion as requisite to national prosperity, of American history as itself sacred, of the millennium as an American affair—notions certainly available to Methodists had they wanted to adopt them—are absent.[21] Instead, more generic precepts occur. In the general fast called for 1796 Methodists were

> To lament the deep rooted vassalage that still reigneth in many parts of these free, independent United States—To call upon the Lord to direct our rulers and teach our senators wisdom—That the Lord would teach our people a just and lawful submission to their rulers—That America may not commit abominations with other corrupt nations of the earth, and partake of their sins and their plagues—[22]

The images of this passage are more evocative of Egypt than the promised land. Such language seems a poor start on an American civil theology.

The accompanying call for a general thanksgiving did speak more positively of the nation. It sought thankful prayers:

> that we have had such faithful, wise and skillful rulers; that we have such good constitutions formed for the respective states—For the general union and government, that this may be kept pure and permanent—For the admirable revolution, obtained and establish[ed] at so small a price of blood and treasure—That religious establishments by law, are condemned and exploded, in almost every spot of this extensive empire.

Even these appear muted, backhanded in comparison with the calls for recognition of Methodism's spread "through the continent of America." Though clearly appreciative of the new government, Methodists reserved their thanksgivings for the land rather than the nation. It was the continent they celebrated:

> To take into remembrance the goodness and wisdom of God displayed towards America, by making it an asylum for those who are distressed in Europe with war and want, and oppressed with ecclesiastic and civil tyranny; the merciful termination of our various wars; the pacifications of the savage tribes; and the rapid settlement and wonderful population of the continent; that we have been able to feed so many thousands, at home and abroad.[23]

Methodists came closer to conceiving the nation in terms analogous to their Reformed compatriots in a sermon preached by John Dow on July 4, 1806. He marshalled the essentials of American political belief—Israel as example; righteousness and piety as requisite to national peace and prosperity; republican government as favorable to religion, truth, and virtue; despotism as strengthening superstition, error, and delusion; American independence as providential; territory, climate, soil, arts, agriculture, trade as blessings.[24] Dow's metaphors presaged Methodist adherence to Christian America and appropriation of its civil theology a decade or so later. Unlike later Methodists, however, Dow left the example of the Hebrews as just that, an example not just for America but for all nations. Israel did not function as type, nor America as antitype. America served no special purpose in God's designs. It enjoyed no covenant relation. Nor did Dow connect Methodism with the nation and place it in national service. Dow called for obedience to God and obedience to government and left the matter there.[25]

Doubtless it was just that prescribed political passivity that made Methodists relatively uninterested in the nature and meaning of the American political experiment. Certainly Coke and Asbury so counseled in their notes on the 1798 Discipline:

> We are debtors to the constitution under which we live (*we, especially in the United States*) for all the blessings of law and liberty which we enjoy: and without a government to support that constitution, all would be anarchy and confusion.[26]

Rendering unto Caesar what was Caesar's, Methodists could then render unto God what was God's. And that, in their view, was the continent.

"The Redeemer Has Planted His Standard in the Midst of Us"

Methodists thought in territorial terms. They did so under what they represent as divine mandate. In the 1798 *Discipline*, bishops Asbury and Coke provided extensive annotations on and scriptural proofs of Methodist belief and practice. Their treatment of America illustrates this territorial imperative. They identified "the sixteen states, and other parts of the continent" as missionary turf. To them "division of the continent" meant for conferences and the itinerancy. They defended the office and authority of episcopacy in terms of its ability to deploy missionaries, allocate ministerial resources and spread revival on a continental basis.[27] The continental imperative made it quite natural for Methodists to ignore political lines. So in 1812 the General Conference could address its members "in the United States of America," and say the following:

> DEARLY BELOVED BRETHREN:—When we retrospect the divine goodness toward us a people, our hearts are animated with sentiments of praise and thanksgiving. We.have been favored with repeated manifestations of the power and grace of God. The Redeemer has planted

his standard in the midst of us, and given astonishing success to our labors, and annually made accessions of thousands to our number. From the cold provinces of Canada to the sultry regions of Georgia— from the shores of the Atlantic to the waters of the Mississippi—in populous cities, improved countries, and dreary deserts, God has extended the triumphs of his grace.[28]

This continental orientation perhaps explains why American—really U.S.—Methodists could be so sensitive about the slightest sign of control from Britain and yet long after independence be quite willing to exercise authority beyond U.S. jurisdiction, in British North America (Canada). The inconsistency did not dawn on Methodists for several decades. It was not so much that American Methodists operated with a double standard as that they operated with a single standard which transcended political lines. That single standard took geographical or continental form because they believed that to be the natural boundary for a holy people.

Asbury and Coke discerned the rationale for the continental orientation. Explicating Methodist behavior, they proclaimed "[O]ur one aim, in all our economy and ministerial labours, is to raise a holy people, crucified to the world and alive to God. . . . " Speaking of ministry, they asserted, "Our original design in forming our religious Society. . . . To raise a holy people. . . . We will have a holy people, or none. In every part of our economy, as well as doctrine, we aim at crucifixion to the world and love to God."[29]

The Prosperity of Zion

If crucified to the world and only submissive to its polity, Methodists permitted their citizenship to rest only metaphorically in the continent. Their true country seems to be indicated in a term that recurs through their journals, a term that actually permitted the metaphorical citizenship in continent. That term was 'Zion'. For Zion they labored; to Zion they belonged. Asbury noted in 1789, "The number of candidates for the ministry are many; from which circumstance I am led to think the Lord is about greatly to enlarge the borders of Zion."[30] In a letter of 1792 he affirmed, "I feel myself uncommonly moved to believe the Lord will give peace to his church, and great prosperity to his Zion this year."[31]

James Haw reported on a Kentucky revival of 1789, "Good news from Zion—The Work of GOD is going on rapidly in the new Western world."[32] Ezekiel Cooper spoke of going "Zionward."[33] Methodists offered *The Methodist Magazine* in the trust that "the work will be found both useful and entertaining to the real friends of Zion." The next year, 1819, they launched the Missionary and Bible Society with an appeal to "the friends of Zion."[34]

Eventually the term took on delimited and denominational significance. Later Methodists equated Zion with American Methodism. The episcopal address of 1824 spoke of "the prosperity of our Zion" and asserted "the borders of our Zion have been enlarged."[35] Bangs would later speak of the "building up our Zion as on a hill"[36] or write "the history of our Zion."[37] But in neither period was 'Zion' a Methodist or an American exclusive. It belonged to the wider evangelical community. And in the earlier period, when Methodists used it, they made an important statement about their citizenship. They placed their membership in a larger ecclesial reality. Hence the 1804 General Conference could greet the British Conference and take notice of missions in Ireland and Wales, "Whenever we hear of the prosperity of Zion, and of the success of the Gospel of our Lord Jesus Christ, it gives us a pleasure far superior to our powers of expression." So Freeborn Garrettson, although speaking at a later date, reflected early Methodist understanding of 'Zion': "I love Zion, for she is my chief joy.—I pray for the militant church wherever scattered, or of whatever sect; but I engaged to confine myself to the people with whom I have lived, and for whom I have spent the prime of my life."[38]

The term 'Zion' performed like the more familiar conception of Methodism's inclusivity, Wesley's 'Catholic Spirit.' But inclusion was only a minor part of its service. Historical yet eschatological, geographic yet missional, organizational yet dynamic, the biblical term 'Zion' connected Methodists with the totality of God's redemptive activity. Zion claimed the sacred past but also the future; it required territory but also purpose; it needed order but also action. It functioned to make the associations implicit in the formula, "the Church, the conference, the continent, and . . . the world." Zion united Methodists with God's people throughout the whole history of redemption, with those they recognized as the godly of their own day, and with the new Jerusalem to come. Asbury made those connections in his year-end meditations for 1802:

> My general experience is close communion with God, holy fellowship with the Father and his Son Jesus Christ, a will resigned, frequent addresses to a throne of grace, a constant serious care for the prosperity of Zion, forethought in the arrangements and appointments of the preachers, a soul drawn out in ardent prayer for the universal Church and the complete triumph of Christ over the whole earth.[39]

Like catholicity, Zion expressed unity. But unlike catholicity, Zion was place; it was people; it was polity; it was redemptive history. Zion gave

Methodists a nation by identifying Methodism with Israel, both old and new. In short, by its identity with Zion, Methodists laid claim to that covenantal relation that gathered in the rich imagery of Old Testament and New.

Hence Methodists who indeed sought the prosperity of Zion would understandably be at a loss to say much meaningful about the new nation. For they had already allocated to a holy people what others would assert of the republic. The Israel which they would build on this continent could not be vested with civil garb. The visible expression of God's New Israel was not state but ecclesia.

A Glass to the Heart?

In restating the single and simple point of this essay, perhaps what was not intended or attempted should be mentioned first. This chapter did not pursue the Americanization of Methodism; Methodist patriotism; Methodist contribution to the American nation, society, or civilization; the extent of Methodist influence; the endeavor to achieve an American Methodist identity; Methodism's establishing itself as a national church.[40] Those topics—which merit attention in their own right and have been much discussed by others—have entered only incidentally into these considerations.

Instead, the topic has been early Methodist conceptions of the nation, the new republic. The argument is simply that Methodists were both highly conscious of and oblivious to it. That paradox derived, at least in part, from their orientation to continent rather than nation and particularly to that polity destined to reign over the continent, Zion. Their order and activity served, as it were, as a glass through which Zion might become visible. As Asbury noted, "All the prospects of the world are dead to me. . . . The glory of the Kingdom of Christ, the organization of a primitive Church of God, these are all my objects; was it possible to set a glass to my heart, you should see them engraven there by the word & spirit of the living God."[41] Asbury's metaphor, strange as it is, makes some sense of Methodist attitudes towards the nation. Methodists invited those who would to look through the nation, to look through them, to the Zion, "the primitive Church of God," that was writ on the Methodist heart. God's kingdom, not American citizenship, was imprinted there.

Second, during these early decades of relative unconcern about the nation, Methodists did become a national church, effectively Americanize, establish the structures and procedures through which their imprint would be placed on America. National organization, identity, and procedure preceded national consciousness. Praxis preceded theory. American

Methodists had a national mission before they conceived it as such. In contrast, the Reformed denominations, heirs to centuries of political reflection and the image-rich Puritan experience, conceived the appropriate relation between religion and the republic, their national mission, and national structures before they institutionalized them. Methodists elaborated a national system of conferences and deployed their ministry on a national basis long before they claimed (Reformed) conceptions of the nation that would give those endeavors American meaning. Orientation to Zion permitted them to proceed without a formal theology of the (American) nation. The Reformed, on the other hand, elaborated quite specific national tasks before their largely local and state societies or the Presbyterian-Congregational Plan of Union were equipped to shoulder them. To reiterate, Methodists became national long before they envisioned or limited their horizons in national terms.

Third, its obliviousness to the nation and reliance upon notions like continent and Zion for corporate purposes left Methodism ill-equipped to think carefully and critically about its societal role and place in the new nation. It gradually absorbed the prevalent public theology and eventually made it very much its own. But it lacked the theological terminology and the habits of mind to assess critically what it appropriated. Methodists simply threw themselves zealously into the building of a Christian America that others had envisioned. Their efforts and the contagion of their missionary style have led historians to denominate the nineteenth century, the Methodist age or Methodist century. Ironically, that reading holds Methodists responsible for nineteenth-century Protestantism's accomplishments—the American civil religion, the identification of Christianity with culture, the imperial style of world missions.[42] It might be argued that Methodism contributed the energy not the design for those "accomplishments." While its vision of Zion certainly mandated effort, Methodism's responsibility really extends further. For it did embrace the design as well, albeit uncritically. There is no doubt that Methodist endeavors did contribute to the Christianization of America; no doubt that by the days of Matthew Simpson, Methodists become outspoken proponents for a Christian society and a civilizing religion; no doubt that by the end of the century Methodists shared in the virtual identification of Christianity with culture. Methodism lacked the terms and disposition to evaluate the public theology.

There is, then, something of an Edenic dimension to these early Methodist self-understandings. Methodists initially conceived their task in culture-transcending terms. The dynamism of the movement doubtless had something to do with such visions. But notions like continent and Zion were intellectually naive, naked, lacking the knowledge of good and evil. When it found itself having to negotiate with the world, Methodism clothed itself with other terms.

Of the early national period we can say that Methodists instead sought the "glory of the Kingdom of Christ, the organization of a primitive Church of God." Were it possible to set a glass to the heart, you should see them engraven there.

4. The Southern Accent of American Methodism

Deeply embedded in Methodist self-consciousness lies a dispute about origins. Did American Methodism begin with Philip Embury in New York or with Robert Strawbridge in Maryland? From the beginning, this controversy over priority has haunted episcopal Methodism, prompting very early efforts at compromise. In 1787, Methodists lodged what looks very much like a compromise formulation in their quasi-constitution, the *Discipline.* In reworking the Wesleyan (British) *Large Minutes* to suit American conditions, the church gave Methodism an American shape by posing a question about its origins. After an initial query concerning "the Rise of Methodism" in Europe, the *Discipline* asked, "What was the Rise of Methodism, so called, in America?" It answered:

> About twenty Years ago, Philip Embury, a local preacher from Ireland, began to preach in the city of New-York, and formed a society of his own Countrymen and the Citizens. About the same time, Robert Strawbridge, a local preacher from Ireland, settled in Frederic County, in the State of Maryland, and preaching there, formed some Societies.

With only minor variations, successive *Disciplines* down to the latest, that of 1988, have repeated that formulation.[1] It is our purpose here to propose that the contest over priority and efforts to mediate it have diverted attention from the more important and underlying question of how region and regional factors shaped Methodism.

Discomfort with Parity

The compromise in the *Discipline* did not suit all concerned with Methodist origins. In 1807 in the first history of American Methodism, "A

47

Comprehensive History of American Methodism,'' rendered in only twenty pages, an English emigrant, southern resident but zealous abolitionist, George Bourne, conceded the case for New York's priority.[2] Another southerner, Jesse Lee, concurred. In his more modestly titled but far more significant and far longer (394 pages) *A Short History of the Methodists,* Lee insisted that "the first permanent Methodist society was formed in the city of New York" and the "first Methodist meeting house . . . built in the United States, was that in New-York."[3]

Other southerners have sought at least the parity achieved in the *Discipline*. In 1859, George C. M. Roberts, then with the American Methodist Historical Society in Baltimore, resolved the issue by pushing both New York and Baltimore origins back to 1760. More typically, Hilary Hudson, in an 1882 volume with the telling title, *The Methodist Armor; Or, A Popular Exposition of the Doctrines, Peculiar Usages, And Ecclesiastical Machinery of the Methodist Episcopal Church, South* retained the formulation of the *Discipline*.[4]

Southern discomfort with parity came to most pointed and forceful expression in the first great history of Methodism from a southern angle, Holland McTyeire's *A History of Methodism*. He insisted: "Robert Strawbridge, both in order of time and talent and service, stands at the head of the noble 'irregulars' who founded Arminian Methodism in America. Embury is worthy of much honor, but the builder of the Log Meeting-house of more."[5] In 1916 that southern view triumphed. Then a Joint Commission on the Origin of American Methodism created by the preceding General Conference of the Methodist Episcopal Church, the (predominantly) northern body of a sectionally divided Methodism, but composed of representatives of that body and the Methodist Episcopal Church, South, and the Methodist Protestant Church, reported back that "to the work of Robert Strawbridge in Maryland belongs the distinction of priority. The New York representatives on this commission complained, quite accurately, that the Church had established procedures that insured a southern or Baltimore majority and a southern conclusion.[6]

Although the tone of Methodist triumphalism and the ferocity of regional competition have abated, the debate over origins continues. Its salience is indicated in the subheadings of the initial chapter in the Baltimore Conference history, *Those Incredible Methodists:*

> The First Class of American Methodism
> The First Dated Transfer of Membership
> The First Meeting House
> Bush—the Second Meeting House

The First American Methodist Deed—Leesburg
The First Recorded Quarterly Conference
The First Methodist Baptism in the World
The First Native Local Preacher
The First Traveling Preacher[7]

Edwin Schell, the author of that chapter, heads us in a fruitful direction by moving beyond the mere issue of priority to the institutional consequences thereof. Earlier, William Warren Sweet, the great mid-century historian of American religion and of Methodism, probed for the implications of Methodism's southern origins. He said:

> American Methodism in its beginnings was very largely a movement within the Southern colonies, and was strongest in Virginia and Maryland. This fact seems to have escaped the attention of most Methodist writers, who have given chief place to the development of early Methodism in the middle colonies.[8]

These comments suggest that the debate over origins both indicates and obscures an important issue. The contest over priority trivializes a much more substantive question about the shaping of early American Methodism. As the title indicates, this essay wishes to ask, not where Methodism started, but where it was decisively molded. The sparring by New York and Baltimore serves to confuse the important issue. The critical matter is not whether Embury preceded Strawbridge, but where Methodism evolved and how its environment affected that evolution. This essay argues for serious reflection about the obvious—that American Methodism developed in the South and has had a southern accent ever since.

Methodism a Southern Religion?

To term Methodism a southern religion is to make a claim about Methodism as a whole. It is argued here that American Methodism has lived for much of its history, perhaps even to this day, with a southern pedigree which, for various reasons, it has chosen to ignore. Such a thesis diverges from accepted findings in both Methodist and southern historiography. Southern religious history has prospered over the last decade, and has done so by breaking with earlier historiographical traditions which had accented the more passive dimensions of southern religion, its culturally determined character; its shaping by an imported evangelicalism; its accommodation to the region, to slavery, to the dominant class. While not obscuring these realities, recent readings also note culturally formative facets of southern religion. Yet none of this more recent literature, so far as I can discern, argues that the South shaped American religion as a whole.[9] Here that note is sounded—southern religion, at least in its Methodist form, may be difficult to distinguish because it imprinted American Methodism as a whole.

Similarly, Methodist historians have tended to observe but pass lightly over the southern character of early Methodism, except to remark upon its deleterious effect on the Methodist conscience and antislavery impulse.[10] They do, generally, recognize the southern prominence of early Methodism. Beyond that they tend not to go. One group of historians, however, has recognized Methodism's southern character: conference historians.

"The Peninsula that lies between the Delaware and Chesapeake bays . . . was the garden of Methodism in America."[11] Citing that claim by Henry Boehm, William Williams entitles his superb history of Delmarva Methodism *The Garden of American Methodism.* Not to be outdone, Edwin Schell enters a counterclaim for Baltimore, calling that area "a fountainhead of the expanding Methodist work."[12] Speaking for Virginia Methodism, Paul Neff Garber affirmed: "It was on the soil of Virginia that much of the American and Methodist tradition was born."[13] Here again, Methodist triumphalism and conference posturing obscure historical patterns. Rather than entering or resolving this squabble, we suggest that all three claims be accepted. For it was there indeed that Methodism took root and the Methodism of these three areas, perhaps with the addition of North Carolina, then expanded to the nation. By early southern Methodism we intend that of the upper South, really that bounded by the Mason-Dixon line, the Methodism which emerged in Chesapeake culture.[14]

Methodism's Southern Contours

In 1775, out of a total Methodist membership of 3,148, 2,384 lived below the Mason-Dixon line. In 1780, owing to the British disruption of the little northern Methodist wing, 7,808 of the movement's 8,504 were southern. By 1784, when the church organized, 13,331 of the total 14,983 were southern. In 1800 the proportions had shifted, but still 45,282 of a total 63,958 were southern. And 122,561 of a total 195,357 Methodists were southern in 1812.

The contours of early Methodism can also be seen in terms of where the church chose to meet. For the first forty years of its organized life, from

1784 to 1824, whenever the church met in a single general conference, whether official or unofficial, it did so in Baltimore. The year 1812 saw an exception to this pattern. The church met that year in New York. During the period in which Methodism experimented with the multiple-session conference, it held those sessions predominantly in the South. In 1785, the first year of this venture, all three sessions convened in the South—at Green Hill's home near Louisburg, North Carolina; in Brunswick county, Virginia; and in Baltimore. In 1788, the conference moved north in seven jumps, Charleston, Georgia, Holstein, Petersburg, Beeson Town, Baltimore and Philadelphia. The year 1790 saw fourteen sessions, only the last three of which lay outside the South—Charleston, Georgia, Kentucky, Holstein, North Carolina, Lane's Chapel, Union Town, Leesburg, Baltimore, Cokesbury, Duck Creek, Philadelphia, Burlington, and New York. In 1796, the church legislated specific boundaries to conferences, thereby giving itself organizational coherence and continuity in territorial terms. The areas encompassed by these conferences once again demonstrate Methodism's southern orientation: New England, Philadelphia, Baltimore, Virginia, South Carolina, and Western.[15]

Other structures of Methodist work bear the same message. A map of circuits for the year 1790, in Lester Cappon's *Atlas of Early American History,* shows us the southern proportions of Methodism. A thin stream of circuits reached up the Hudson, with a slight branch, as it were, over to Boston. The major current of Methodism flowed from Trenton in the north due west and from Savannah in the south, northwest.[16] The same proportions appear in data Jesse Lee collected in 1799 about the number of local preachers. These numbers indicate where Methodism possessed leadership strength and potential. Of the 850 total, 671 were southern.[17] The obituaries in the *Minutes* disclose the lavish spending of that southern contribution. Of the 245 ministers who had died by 1829, the nativity of 212 is clearly indicated. Virginia produced 45, Maryland 33, and North Carolina 23, almost half the total.[18]

Migration of Southern Methodism

Actually, the southern accent in Methodism was even greater than the data above indicate. The proportion of southerners to northerners altered less than the raw statistics imply and the church slipped northward demographically (rather than simply geographically) more gradually than the additional northern conferences and circuits northward suggest. The numbers and contours of organizational life understate the southern ethos of

Methodism, for just before and after the turn of the century, Virginia, Maryland, the Peninsula—the Methodist stronghold—lost people, Methodists among them, who fled slavery and spent soil. Many of these southerners moved into areas that would be counted on the northern side of the ledger: Ohio and later Indiana and Illinois.

Asbury's journal provides vivid, personal meaning to this movement. In 1807 he wrote of finding lodging in Ohio with "Andrew M'Grew, lately from Baltimore county, Maryland."[19] Two years later he dined at "Philip Davis's: This is an old Virginia family, and here as brethren and sisters whom I have known, some twenty, others above thirty years."[20] He called this area "New Virginia." For example, in 1812, in the context of reflections about charges lodged against him for ordaining a slave and a Virginian's refusal to manumit, Asbury mused, "Old Virginia, because of the great emigrations westward, and deaths, decreases in the numbers she gives to the Methodists; but New Virginia gains."[21] He seemed to reflect about Old Virginia when in New and about New Virginia when in Old.[22] Similarly, Asbury found that original southern Methodism in western parts of the South proper. For instance, in 1805, in Kentucky, he noted:

> Saturday, 21 September . . . We visited Daniel Grigg. I found several of my old friends at this place—among them Colonel Barratt of Alleghany, and his wife; Mrs. Tittle, and some from Baltimore county, and the State of Delaware—and thus our people are scattered abroad; but, thank the Lord! they are still in the fold, and on their way to glory. . . . Monday, 23 September. I visited John Vernon, an early member of society, at Lewis Afree's, near Duck Creek, State of Delaware. I must look up our old sheep and lambs.[23]

Asbury visited the just mentioned Colonel Barratt again in 1811, in the state of Ohio.[24] Patterns of communication also disclose the southern movement west and the continuing power of the ties to Old Virginia. Those larger dimensions of the South pervade that remarkable collection of letters between the Virginian Edward Dromgoole and his network, many of whom had moved to Ohio.[25]

What Asbury and Dromgoole observed on a personal level, we can see on a corporate scale in the leadership of the conference created to gather in the wandering southerners. In 1804 the secretary of this Western Conference (comprised of Ohio, Kentucky, Cumberland, and Holston districts) caught the southern character of the Methodist West. He minuted states of origin for some of those taken in on trial. Two thirds came from the South.[26]

The states of origin should indicate that we must think of this early southern Methodism as dynamic and expanding. The church as a whole moved west—lay folk, exhorters, local preachers, and those aspiring to the itinerancy. That hoary Methodist commonplace that the itinerant won the West distorts the picture. The itinerant found Methodism already there but receptive to leadership and to the Methodist connectional system. We need a rewritten version of Methodist history, seen from the bottom up. From that grass-roots vantage, as the above indicates, the South provided leadership for the expanding church.

The same pattern can be seen in terms of national elites. There as at all other levels the South dominated. The South provided the national leadership for Methodism. The presiding elders—the effective supervisors, educators, justices, administrators for the church—overwhelmingly hailed from the South. In 1800, for instance, seventeen presiding elders superintended the itinerating preachers across the nation. Their origins:

Benjamin Blanton, southern (according to Asbury)
Francis Poythress, Virginia
Jonathan Jackson, North Carolina
William McKendree, Virginia
Enoch George, Virginia
Daniel Hitt, Virginia
Christopher Spry, Virginia or Maryland
Thomas Ware, New Jersey
Joseph Everett, Maryland
Solomon Sharp, Maryland
William McLenahan, Ireland
Freeborn Garrettson, Maryland
Shadrach Bostwick, Maryland
John Brodhead, Pennsylvania
Joseph Jewell, apparently Delaware, where made deacon
George Pickering, Maryland
Joshua Taylor, New Jersey[27]

The southern character of the leadership cadre is unmistakable. Thirteen of the presiding elders came from the South, three from the North and one from Ireland.

Perhaps we might think of Methodism as the religious culture that southerners took to the continent—as for example what Freeborn Garrettson took from Maryland to Nova Scotia and New York, what Jesse Lee took from Virginia to New England, what Richard Allen took from Delaware to Philadelphia, what William McKendree took from Virginia west, what Ezekiel Cooper took from the Peninsula to Pennsylvania, New Jersey, and New York, what Philip Gatch took from Maryland to Ohio, and what Peter Cartwright took from Virginia into Kentucky, Ohio, Indiana, and Illinois.

Admittedly, we only discern a dominant tone, one that had to compete with other notes, both from within and without the Wesleyan tradition and from various sources in the culture. So it must be conceded that Methodism was also what Thomas Ware took from New Jersey to Tennessee. Still to speak metaphorically, southerners wrote early Methodist history. And to speak literally rather than metaphorically, it was quite fitting that the Virginian and national leader, Jesse Lee, wrote the first full-scale Methodist history.[28] Methodism belonged in a rather special sense to the South.

The Southern Shape of American Methodism: Some Hypotheses

This argument varies from and yet ultimately contributes to three important trends in the recent historiography of southern Methodism. All three trends are integrative or holistic. One views southern Methodism within the larger Methodist or Wesleyan tradition. A second treats Methodism as part of the distinctive southern interplay of religion and culture. The third attends to the manifold complexity and interconnectedness of evangelicalism as a national phenomenon, and includes southern religion.[29] Here we begin by isolating Methodism in the South from its northern (as well as British) expression but conclude with a national Methodism, albeit with one far more 'southern' than the traditional estimate. Second, for purposes of viewing the way in which a southern ethos permeates a distinct tradition, we isolate Methodism somewhat arbitrarily from other variants of southern religion. Third, by positing its role in shaping Methodism nationally, we may open up again the issue of what constitutes evangelical culture and question the longstanding habit of tracing American religious patterns to New England origins.[30]

What then may be said about early southern Methodism and Methodism's southern accent? The movement's southern origins stamped five facets of early Methodism. Each gave a peculiar accent, a peculiar way of talking, a peculiar set of concerns to Methodism. For the most part, these facets receive more extensive discussion elsewhere in this volume. They deserve reiteration here for their connection to the South. For through them, Methodism would continue to give voice to southern concerns. And yet in each case, the movement increasingly lost the capacity to hear the accent in these concerns.

Early southern Methodism offered an antipatriarchal, evangelical Anglicanism; evidenced a deep ambivalence over slavery; constructed the church on a biracial basis; conceived of Methodist purpose in territorial terms; and dramatized grace in large, public events.

An Evangelical Alternative to Patriarchal Anglicanism

First, as Rhys Isaac, Bertram Wyatt-Brown, and Donald Mathews have argued, the eighteenth-century evangelicalism of Baptists and Methodists defined itself over against the norms, beliefs, and folkways of the patriarchal culture of Anglican, slaveholding gentility.[31] An excerpt from Stith Mead's route to Methodism dramatizes that new self-definition:

> Jan. 1790—Mr. Samuel Mead, a brother next youngest to me, who appears to be a sincere penitent for his sins, and myself travelled to the State of Georgia, to see our relations, whose god is in this world, with the rich and fashionable gay. I strove to encourage my brother, as I was a believer unto salvation, and he was only a seeker of religion. In Feb. we arrived in Georgia, and was received with much persecution from many of our relations, who soon raised a dancing party, when my brother was caught in the snare of Satan—I was much persuaded to stay and partake with them, but refused; having several miles to ride to Col. A. Gordon's, a brother-in-law, where I lived. My sisters often danced before me, others suggested I was deranged, and soon would be raving mad—but blessed be God, in the midst of all my temptations and trials, I find him to be a "friend that sticketh by me, nigher than a brother." I often took up my cross with a trembling hand, to pray in my father's family.[32]

Today, many would dismiss as petty, individualistic moralism Mead's portrayal of central features of genteel culture—like dancing—as the snare of Satan. It was an attitude that was quite as strange to some of Mead's contemporaries, including those who knew him best. His posture struck his relations as madness.

Isaac and Mathews recover the force of that contemporary estimation but invert its valuation. They construe this defiance of gentility as explosive, radical, Christian egalitarianism empowering the lowly of the society to defy the dominant power structure. The combative, antiworldly, antigentry, antipatriarchal rhetoric functioned, argue Mathews and Isaac, to create and sustain a powerful, alternative community. Within this new community, women and men, the lowly and the mighty, blacks and whites experienced a grace that made it possible to affirm one another. Mathews employs the text preached on by Freeborn Garrettson and reported by Asbury, "Disallowed Indeed of Men, but Chosen of God and Precious," as theme and chapter title through which to capture this radical phase of evangelicalism.[33]

As we have seen, this egalitarian spirit found institutional expression in the communal structures of Methodism. It found voice in its Wesleyan and particularly in its vernacular rhetoric. The radical accent to early Methodism was doubtless largely accidental. Methodists came to speak for the lowly because it was the lowly that initially gave them a hearing. Further, the foil of gentility, a referent for Wesley and British Methodism as well, took on a sharper edge in southern society where gentility presented itself as the order of the world and was not enveloped in the finely graded social hierarchy of Britain. The way Methodism presented itself and the success it enjoyed in the South also had much to do with the movement's emergence during the revolutionary epoch. Though its egalitarianism differed in premise, shape, and purpose from that which gave shape to the nation, Methodism nevertheless capitalized on its peculiar universalistic and Arminian democratic appeal. For these reasons and perhaps others, early Methodism accented its gospel with a radical social critique, an attack on the social conventions of the ruling class, the elaboration of an alternative moral code.

While Methodists joined with Baptists in defiance of this Anglican patriarchalism, they differed in strategy. Baptists offered ritual, creed, polity, and ethic which virtually inverted Anglicanism. Methodists defied the Anglican culture of patriarchalism in more insidious fashion. Methodism countered Anglican patriarchy by offering itself as a surrogate, before 1784 as a reform movement within the Anglican Church, after 1784 as a clear alternative. Here was an Anglican cultus that symbolized independence not the crown, equality not patriarchy, freedom not slavery. Methodists advanced, as William Williams has argued, because they provided southerners brought up with the prayer book "a second 'English' church." "It is no accident," says Williams, "that on the Peninsula and elsewhere in early America, Methodism had its greatest success in areas previously dominated by the Church of England and the descendants of Englishmen."[34] Williams helps put into proper perspective the argument advanced by Frank Baker and others that American Methodism continued far more of the belief and cultus of Wesleyanism and Anglicanism than Americans have appreciated.[35] Conceding that, we then need to recognize that however continuous in substance early Methodism was with British Wesleyanism and with Anglicanism on either side of the Atlantic, Americans employed this British religious system to differentiate themselves from the world of slaveholding, patriarchal Anglicanism. Hence we need to view the Methodist system and Methodist strictures against worldliness together as a complex code of alternative belief and alternative behavior defining a new community. That code, given initially to the slave culture of the Chesapeake, became a national pattern.

The code did, however, lose much of its import in transmission. The taboos, the prohibitions against dancing and gambling, the moralism traveled north and west better than the egalitarian spirit and ethical critique to which they gave point and expression. That southern accent was easily lost. Several factors frustrated transmission. First, this egalitarian code was highly contextual, defined over against the slave-holding elites and plausible at a point when they were on the defensive. This gospel lost something when taken out of context and when the context itself changed. Second, this gospel was borne by Methodist language, and particularly its vernacular rhetoric, which Methodists never codified or gave official standing to. The itinerants continued to preach its terms, but the meanings gradually shifted. Third, the code transmitted more readily both in time and space than the alternative community that it was intended to create did. In consequence, what Methodism eventually heard of this early egalitarianism were just the taboos—the thou shalt nots, not dance, not gamble, not drink—the moralisms. The richer southern accent dissipated.

In the South, as Mathews has shown, evangelicalism eventually captured the elites and the genteel culture it had once despised. In that accommodation to culture, it preserved style not substance—the moralistic lifestyle but not the radical, egalitarian community. A similar accommodation, we suspect, occurred, perhaps even more rapidly, in the transmission of this southern evangelicalism north and northwest. Away from its primary referent, the patriarchal culture, grounded in Wesley's rules of the *Discipline,* and cohering with the pronounced legalism of American culture as a whole, Methodist moralism readily became an end in itself. Furthermore, early Methodist aversion to genteel patriarchalism did not automatically translate itself into egalitarian authority structures within Methodism, though some within the movement thought it should. Many would chafe under the authority vested in the episcopacy, an authority largely exercised over and limited to the traveling ministry, but nevertheless in some tension with the more egalitarian aspects of Methodism. The secession of the Republican Methodists drained out some of these folk, the later departure of the Methodist Protestants others. Both attested the continuing appeal of these sentiments and their minority status within Methodism as a whole.

Yet Methodists could never divorce themselves entirely from the radical messages latent in Methodist rhetoric and lifestyle. Black Methodists never did.[36] For whites, these impulses would resurface, albeit in different form, in reform movements, the Holiness cause, and women's organizations.

Ambivalence over Slavery

Second, American Methodism derived from its southern beginnings a deep ambivalence about slavery and the Black. This has to be one of the most canvassed of all Methodist topics. Much of the *specifically Methodist* discussion has been structured around conference legislation on slavery. Northern and Black historians have read this story as Methodist principle compromised and southern interest honored.[37] Southerners have construed that legislation, as did A. T. Bledsoe in 1871, as an expression of a "British conscience . . . sensitive, if not morbid," on the subject of slavery and as imposed by the British leadership.[38] Both interpretations tend to locate the commitment to antislavery outside the South and to depict southerners as quite ready to embrace slavery. Early statements by Jesse Lee and others do lend themselves to such constructions. However, such viewpoints, standard in Methodist historiography, overlook the overwhelmingly southern character of the church during this early period and fail to recognize early antislavery as itself a southern impulse. They also fail therefore to appreciate the complexity of Methodist antislavery sentiment. It came laced with racism.

Journal entries, however, clearly illustrate both an inclusion and an exclusion of Blacks, antislavery commitment and racism. For a quarterly meeting in 1785, Ezekiel Cooper recorded, after love feast at 9:00: "Then preaching, in and out of doors, began at twelve o'clock. Brother Whatcoat preached within, Brother Cloud outside. George Moore gave an exhortation in, and Harry a black man, exhorted without. It was a good time."[39] Four years later James Meacham complained of "the prejudice of Education. [W]e can't have the privelege [sic] of meeting the Blacks in the Church." He noted that they listened at the window. A couple of years later he recorded his hope to see the poor slaves in Heaven and "their cruel bloody oppressive Masters . . . burn in Hell fire for ever & ever."[40] How should we construe such entries? Initially southern Methodists (and Methodists outside the South) found slavery and the treatment of the slave to be a metaphor of the world as ruled by Satan. Not surprisingly, some Methodists, southerners included, attacked slavery and called the Black to draw near. From that impulse derived the important eighteenth-century public pronouncements and conference legislation on slavery. However, the same folk had difficulty in welcoming Blacks fully into the household of faith and left them to listen through the window. Or, as Cooper reported for the Calvert quarterly meeting in 1791, they were sent to the barn.

Entries from personal journals—from Joseph Pilmore in 1771 onward—depict this strange ambivalence.[41] So also does correspondence. A probing letter from an ex-Virginian in Ohio answering his friend Edward Dromgoole in Virginia illustrates that troubled inner state, its southern rootage, and its transmission north. The friend noted Droomgoole's "pilgrimage to the Land of reste," but probed his dissatisfaction with "the land where you now are." Weighing reasons for relocation to "the Land of Liberty," the friend thought financial considerations insufficient. However, if it is

> because you live in a land of Slavery and have you[r] doubts whether it be right in the sight of God for you to die there and live [leave] your children and grand ch[i]l[dren] In that land of oppression, When there is a fare [far] more excellent place provided and that you might be the happy instrument under God to plant them in this good land Where that evil is not and from every possible circumstance the free born sons Of Ohio will never admit it [slavery]. If this be the cause I say Come in the Name of the Lorde.[42]

So what southern Methodists transmitted to the nation was not a British conscience, nor a compromise-prone conscience, nor a racism-free conscience, but a troubled conscience. Here, too, the resonances that gave meaning, texture, and feeling to that conscience were less readily passed on than the specific legislative acts about slaves and slavery.

In consequence, later Methodism remembered a specific stand that it had once taken on slavery without remembering its (southern) social context or the ambivalences with which it had been rendered. Later reformers easily envisioned a past more radical than it had been and construed their own contemporaries and the ambivalences about racial matters of that latter day as betraying the Methodist heritage. In fact, Methodists typically passed on this troubled conscience quite readily and faithfully but could not hear the resonances it had with the past.

A Biracial Church

Third, and in consequence of the overtures to Blacks, early southern Methodism launched itself as a biracial movement. Despite the segregation, the racism and the rapid capitulation to the slave interests, early

Methodism made a sufficiently credible appeal to Blacks for them to continue in uneasy relation with the movement. William McKendree said of a 1790 quarterly meeting what so many other preachers echoed, "Brother Paup preached to the white congregation; I went into the grove with the Black people, and of a truth Jesus was there."[43] Such entries suggest that something quite dramatic happened when Blacks heard the Methodist gospel. At any rate, Blacks responded. In 1786, the first year of count by race, the *Minutes* show 1,890 Black members. By 1797, 12,215 Blacks belonged, 5,106 in Maryland, 2,490 in Virginia and 2,071 in North Carolina, approximately one-quarter of total membership. Blacks both appropriated and transformed Methodism. In early leaders like Harry Hosier, Richard Allen, and Henry Evans, we see the standardbearers of an unnumbered line of Black religious leaders, who, in the slave South as well as in the North, became the effective transmitters of Methodism to the Black folk. In that appropriation and transmission, as Albert Raboteau has sensitively shown, Blacks nuanced Evangelicalism with African religious culture.[44]

To this obvious pattern, we would append a somewhat less obvious implication. To recognize the denomination as biracial confers legitimacy, perhaps even primary legitimacy, on Black Methodism. What Donald Mathews has suggested for southern religion generally then applies obviously to Methodism, namely that southern Methodism and Methodism nationally have to be seen as both Black and white. While the two forms diverged, they did so from shared origins.[45] The point is made with white Methodists in mind; others will doubtless concede it readily. In important respects, Black Methodists—African Methodist Episcopal, African Methodist Episcopal Zion, Christian Methodist Episcopal as well as those within United Methodism—may preserve and represent Methodism more faithfully than white.

That representation may be fullest in the vernacular that Blacks found a vehicle for—the spiritual. Spirituals gave voice to a religious culture that was distinctively Black and African. The spirituals may also transmit important accents of a religiosity shared by Black and white—its southern accent.

Purpose in Territorial Terms

The fourth characteristic can be seen in relation to the purpose American Methodists, following Wesley, set for themselves. The first *Discipline* asked: "What may we reasonably believe to be God's design in raising up the Preachers called *Methodists*? A. To reform the Continent, and to spread scriptural Holiness over these lands." After 1790, the bishops incorporated this statement of purpose into their prefatory address.[46] There it remained through much of the nineteenth century, carrying the endorsement of subsequent bishops. Another chapter argues that historians have seriously misled us by anachronistically reading into that language understandings of reform applicable more to the reformers of the 1830s, 1890s, or 1970s.[47] They have done so by construing Methodist antislavery, and perhaps the abortive attempts to lobby the Virginia legislature, as emblematic of the reformist dimensions of a Wesleyan commitment to social holiness. Then they chart a Methodist retreat from this reforming program and spirit, a retreat from collective resolve into individualism and from piety and reform into piety alone. That retreat historians epitomize with a statement made by Bishop William McKendree in an episcopal address in which he changed the statement of Methodist purpose ever so subtly. He substituted a preposition for a conjunction. Instead of affirming with Wesley and the *Discipline* that God's design for the Methodists was to reform the continent *and* spread scriptural holiness, he spoke of reforming *by* spreading scriptural holiness, thus putting Methodist emphasis on holiness. Such a construction of McKendree's formulation and of Methodist retreat into piety hinges on construing the antislavery of early Methodism as though it were a reform impulse of the 1830s.

However, had one asked an early Methodist, particularly a southerner fervidly committed to rooting out slavery, what he or she meant by reforming the continent, one would have heard familiar rhetoric about piety, discipline, and godly behavior—touching *both corporate and individual life* and certainly touching both slave and slaveholder. One would not have heard what we now would think of as reform. The reason for this has much to do with the southern and Anglican origins of Methodism (it also had much to do with their deeper origin in Mr. Wesley's political sensitivities). Put most directly and in comparative terms, southern Methodists lacked what was prominent in the religious discourse of both New England and the upper Middle Colonies, namely a *public theology*. Eventually, Methodists adopted one, thanks in no small measure to the critics of episcopacy and interpreters of the Methodist legacy like Nathan Bangs. By the middle third of the nineteenth century they would speak in eloquent terms about a Christian nation, God's purposes therein, how Methodists might reform America so as to bring it into accord with God's will, and how such reforms could be achieved educationally, socially, and politically. For the most part, early Methodists did not theorize in such terms. And again the largely southern and Anglican dimensions of Methodism have much to do with this.

The easiest way to explain Methodist reform is to say that Methodists were neither Calvinists nor Commonwealthmen. Such discourse, after all, derived from New England Puritanism and radical Whiggery. Methodists experienced this rhetoric in the Revolution, in confrontations with Presbyterians, and in the Enlightenment wing of colonial Anglicanism. None of those encounters was, for Methodists, positive. Hence we do not find Methodists preaching anything like the the election sermons of New England. Instead, they conceived of their purposes in territorial not political terms. They spoke of continent not nation. To view them as concerned only with the individuals and only with their spiritual lives, however, badly misconstrues them. They had a very powerful corporate purpose and did, in fact, offer a model of a reformed continent. They sustained it with no theory and they gave it a name we would never use for reform—conference.

Grace Dramatized in Public Events

The fifth and final characteristic gave substance to that vision for a reformed continent, but also to the other Methodist 'southern' patterns. The 'conference' that Methodists offered southerners and then Americans generally functioned initially as an institutionalization of radical egalitarian community. As we have seen in earlier chapters, conference and particularly the quarterly conference served as a context within which to deal with slavery, as a social form permitting two races to live together, and as a way of reforming the continent. What early southern Methodism offered Americans as its model of the church, its vision of the corporate life, its foretaste of a reformed continent had a different character initially than it would in the two forms into which it transformed itself in the nineteenth century—the structure of governing conferences and the camp meeting.[48]

In its earliest form, this system of Methodist conferences and particularly the quarterly meeting takes on great significance, and not just administrative significance, when viewed in its southern context. The quarterly meeting served as a corporate drama in which Methodists acted out for themselves and the world what they saw as God's invitation to Christian discipleship.

The pattern before 1784, Freeborn Garrettson described for a Bolingbroke quarterly meeting of August 19, 20, 1780: preaching and quarterly business on the 19th, then love feast at 9:00 and preaching at 11:00 on the 20th. He noted:

> It appeared as if the whole country came together at 11:00 o'clock. I think at least there was between two and three thousand. Four of us

preached and one exhorted. Glory be to God, Bolingbroke never saw
such a day before. I think the devil's kingdom was well shaken.

The preaching continued for the next two days.[49] After 1784, the newly
organized Methodist Episcopal Church began the second day with love
feast; followed with eucharist, preaching, sometimes baptisms or memorial services (following or interspersed as appropriate); and concluded
with more preaching. The other Garrettson, Richard, captured some of
the drama of the second day of a Petersburg quarterly meeting of 1788:

> The next day we met at nine o'clock to administer the sacrament, and
> whilst this was doing in the house, we went into the woods to preach
> to those that did not communicate. I suppose we had about one thou-
> sand and five hundred. . . . [T]he power of God fell down on the peo-
> ple, and such bitter lamentations were heard, that I was obliged to
> desist. . . .
>   In the evening we got as many of the mourners together as we could,
> and put them under an arbour. I went into the pulpit, and looked down
> through a window (they being under it).[50]

As we have noted in the prior chapters, we better understand these
large crowds, the cadre of preachers, the feast of Methodist events, the
dramatic encounter of church with world, the consequent revivals, if we
see them in Chesapeake context. Both Rhys Isaac and John Stilgoe have
shown us that community there differed radically from that of New England or the Pennsylvania–New Jersey area. The Puritans defined community spatially in towns built around church and commons. The diverse
communities of the middle colonies legitimated themselves and recognized pluralism by defining community in neighborhoods. In the Chesapeake, community quite literally occurred. Events rather than towns or
affinity-group neighborhoods served to establish and legitimate southern
life together. Southerners defined and dramatized their community by
gathering for social, political, military, leisure, business, and religious purposes.[51] In quarterly meeting, Methodists offered southerners an alternative to the worldly forms of community.

The southern marks on conference have been largely overlooked primarily because of the way in which conference evolved. First, when na-
tionalized and ritualized, this southern form of community became known
as camp meeting. And the 'western' camp meeting rather than the South-
eastern quarterly meeting has been traditionally recognized as the typical
Methodist drama.[52] Second, as the conference system evolved into the
primary modality of Methodist administration, it lost many of its 'southern' communal features. By its transformation from a model of Christian

community into an administrative system on the one hand and staged camp meetings on the other, conference masked its southern origins.

Conclusion: The Loss of the Southern Accent

Here, then, are five important accents of early southern Methodism, accents later of Methodism nationally—

> an evangelical Anglicanism, defined over against but continuing and transforming the Anglicanism of patriarchy and gentility;
> a deep ambivalence over slavery;
> biracial church membership;
> the conception of Methodist purposes in territorial rather than political terms; and
> the offering of religious community as a large public event in which God's offer of salvation could be dramatized.

Readers of Mathews's *Religion in the Old South* know that this radical phase of evangelicalism was a casualty of its own successes. In winning the southern elites, it came to terms with power, culture, caste. And white southerners not only lost their accent, they forgot they ever heard it. Later racial and regional church politics further dimmed the memory. For their part, northern Methodists had no interest in discovering the southern roots of their commitments. And southerners who bitterly condemned the northern political church had even less interest in recovering their pre-political but radical past. Only the Blacks remembered; they did so by putting it to song.

The Methodist Episcopal Church, South, preserved in its first and early *Disciplines* the episcopal address which set forth "a brief account of the rise of Methodism both in Europe and America" and also Section I "Of the Origin of the Methodist Episcopal Church." These functioned to sustain the South's claim to be in legitimate continuity with early Methodism, a point repeated *ad nauseam* in southern apologetics. The church added a section on the origin of the Methodist Episcopal Church, South. The former covered the saga leading up to 1784; the latter concerned the division of the church North and South in 1844. The juxtaposed treatments achieved the desired result of connecting the 1844 church with primitive Methodism.[53] It did so by obliterating sixty years of southern Methodist history. And with it went the southern accent of American Methodism. All that remained was a contest over priorities, as between Strawbridge and Embury.

5. Conference as a Means of Grace

The first historian of American Methodism gave the movement its narrative structure. Jesse Lee set out the Methodist story as conference. That structure is evident in his chapter titles:

"From the first society . . . to the first conference."
"From the first conference in 1773, to the conference in 1779."
"From the year 1779, to the time of our being formed into a regular church in 1784."
"From the first general conference in 1784, to the end of the year 1786."[1]

This overall dramatic shape of the volume informed the internal dynamic of the chapters and the actual telling of the story. Within the chapters, Lee traced developments and action from one conference to the next. "1774.—The second conference," he recounted, "was held this year in Philadelphia, on the 25th day of May."[2] Two pages later, he reported, "In 1775, the third conference was held on May 17, in Philadelphia."[3] And so the story unfolded. Methodist histories, particularly early ventures like Lee's, structured time from conference to conference, sketched expansion in terms of the addition of discrete conferences, and analyzed governance as the elaboration of a hierarchy of conferences.[4]

It was a narrative structure that Lee must have found axiomatic and that his contemporaries relied upon for their journals and diaries.[5] Moreover, it is a narrative structure that subsequent Methodist historians have found difficult to resist. The Methodist saga seems almost inevitably, naturally, appropriately, to unfold from one conference to the next.

Lee did not invent this narrative form. History-as-conference, conference-as-history derives from Wesley and belongs to the wider Wesleyan movement. It is a staple of Methodist reflection, both individual and corporate.[6] Conference is a modality of Methodist thought because conference defines the Methodist movement in some quite fundamental ways.[7] Here the focus falls on the how it defines American Methodism. The main points bear particularly on the annual conference, the basic unit of Methodist structure, but also relate, though somewhat less directly, to two other levels of structure, both of which are also conference—the quarterly meeting and, after it emerged in 1792, the general conference.[8]

The Multivalence of Conference

Conference measures Methodist time. As Lee grasped, Methodist time falls out in specific units, from one conference to the next. That is the duration of an appointment; that the period in which a given circuit claims a particular preacher; that the rhythm of church life as a whole. At conference, the entire movement—whether small or large—takes on specific form as leaders are connected to people. And then at the next conference, the movement acquires new form. Methodism exists, quite literally, from conference to conference. The conference defines Methodist time. Hence the ease with which Methodist historians fall back upon conference for periodization and as the narrative structure of their accounts.

Conference came eventually to define Methodist space as well.[9] When that happened, the rhythms of conference time were made specific to a given geographic area. That superimposition of the reality of conference on territory, on the American landscape, had much to do with the sheer size of the American continent and the way in which Methodism penetrated the American wilderness. It also had something to do with the fact that Methodism emerged in the Chesapeake, where communal existence had a peculiarly temporal spatiality to it.[10] The identification of conference with territory rested finally upon a specific decision made in 1796. In that year, as Lee observed: "[O]ur whole connection was divided into six yearly conferences."[11] Thereafter, the word 'conference' defined Methodist space. Indeed, an adjective was needed to specify which space— New England, Philadelphia, Baltimore, Virginia, South Carolina, Western.[12] And that particular spatial character of conference has made its own claim on the historical imagination. Its expression is the conference history. As any student of Methodism will know, such conference histories—of the Baltimore Conference, the Philadelphia Conference, the Virginia Conference, etc.—abound. These and the conference journals on which they are largely based constitute the overwhelming bulk of most library collections with strong Methodist holdings. They illustrate the way conference defined Methodist space.

From the very beginning of the American movement—indeed, of the British movement—conference also had a specific social meaning as well. Conference identified a body of preachers called Methodist. Over time its social specificity increased. When the initially one conference first divided into several conferences, the bishop(s) moved preachers between conferences freely and established the membership of a given conference by summoning persons to it. As the territory became geographically fixed, so did membership. Gradually, preachers came to belong to a given conference and, over the course of the nineteenth century, as the church became more regional, movement between conferences became less frequent. Simple belonging delineated social meaning, but other factors, the other functions of conference, defined its character. Among them, of note, were the claims conference made on its members (claims initially those of Wesley on the body of preachers which he brought into being and into connection with himself); its prominence as the engine of Methodist activity; the increased use of it (from Wesley's day on) for legislative, judicial, and administrative purposes; and its emergence as the central structure and the primary administrative agency of American Methodism. Its very multivalence, the multiple roles played through membership in it, increased the intensity of that belonging.[13] Through that intensity, as we have seen in chapter 1, conference became something of a fraternal order.

Conference's fraternal character presents itself in the "bro" or "brother" language the preachers used of one another, terms recurrent throughout their journals. Those terms are striking in the salutations and feelings expressed in letters. Expressions like the following recur through "The Letters Written to Daniel Hitt, Methodist Preacher, 1788 to 1806":

> I take this opportunity to salute you, Dear Bro. though we are parted in body, yet [ink spot] we are one in Spirit, for my part the distance which separates us, seems to increase the ties of friendship, which makes me, that I seldom bow before the throne of Grace without makeing mention of you, that we may be co-workers together here, & co-heirs of the Kingdom of Glory.[14]

Fraternal feelings and expectations recur also for the descriptions of the gatherings of preachers, particularly the conferences. Asbury, for instance, took the fraternal temperature of the conferences. Those that had gone well earned a notation like "all ended in love and peace."[15] Boehm rendered similar judgments. He described his own Philadelphia Conference's session of 1808 as "like one great love-feast from beginning to end." His fraternal feeling for this body was well expressed in a comment for the following year, "It was a privilege to see my brethren, 'true yoke-fellows. . . . ' "[16] That fraternal dimension Thomas Ware recalled quite vividly: "[T]hose happy days of primitive Methodism, when a young and growing band of Christians and Christian ministers were labouring together in the common cause, and united by feelings of Christian sympathy and affection infinitely stronger than the ties of blood"[17] Conference also served, then, to delineate social boundaries and social realities. Conference was and is a social term.[18]

Conference has also served as the Methodist mode of order. This, its most familiar function, is what most Methodists would think of when the term 'conference' is used.[19] Conference has to do with polity, with church order. American Methodism ordered and structured itself through conferences—the quarterly meeting that gathered together the societies and preachers for a circuit, the annual conference composed of all the traveling preachers, and eventually the general conference that evolved into a quadrennial delegated assembly. In the Methodist lexicon, 'conference' refers to such bodies of preachers (eventually of laity as well) that exercise executive, legislative, and judicial functions for the church or some portion thereof. Established by John Wesley, the British conference remained his creature during his lifetime but on his death inherited much of his decision-making and policy-setting authority. It became a central feature, perhaps the central feature, of Methodist polity, on both sides of the Atlantic. For the American church, conference's political dimensions have been often noted and measured. Indeed, the drama in Methodist histories typically derives from conference, its struggle to political competence and the ongoing struggles between conference and episcopacy for authority and power.[20] When analyzed or indexed, 'conference' has that polity meaning. Unfortunately, it frequently bears that meaning alone.[21] But, as we have already indicated, 'conference' possessed a richer significance in Methodist life and discourse than the lexicon admits. And yet, conference was and became ever more the Methodist mode of order.

Conference served also in some respects, as we have seen, as the Methodist way of being 'church'. This, perhaps its most important function, may also be its least appreciated. Prior to the Christmas Conference of 1784, Methodists struggled with but for the most part sustained Wesley's commitment to remain a leavening movement within the Church of England. Expressive of that commitment was Methodist reliance upon the Anglican Church for the sacraments. For these, Methodists repaired to the local parish of the Church of England. That—the Anglican Church in both its local and national expression—Methodists recognized as 'church'. They were not 'church', but a reform movement within.

That commitment to respect the Church and to keep their own endeavors in proper relation thereunto guided colonial American Methodists as well. However, despite that commitment, American Methodists found themselves usurping and verging on ecclesial status. They behaved most like a church and functioned in a very 'catholic' fashion when they gathered in quarterly meeting. There the entire range of leadership and membership participated in the full array of Methodist services. Something of the nature of the event can be seen in the quarterly meeting reported by Freeborn Garrettson for April 1780:

> Monday 17 [18]—I set out this morning very early with my dear friends to quarterly meeting. Blest be God it appeared as if the whole country came together. Our meeting held about three hours. I was much pleased, I think good was done in my Master's name.
> Tuesday 18 [19]—Our love feast began about eight o'clock, it was a love feast to many precious souls. Public meeting began at 12 o'clock. The Rev. Mr. Megan read prayers and the Rev. Mr. Neal . . . delivered a very warm discourse. I held forth after him and Brother Asbury concluded the meeting. Glory be to the Lord, I think I never saw a more powerful time in my life, blest be my God, many seemed to be groaning for redemption in the blood of a crucified Jesus. Oh my soul is in raptures, I want words to utter the praises of my dear Lord, and Savior Jesus Christ.[22]

The two reverends here were Anglican clergy in sympathy with the Methodist movement. Their presence, that of the other Methodist leadership from the circuit, and a full schedule of religious services made the quarterly meeting very church-like. Prior to 1784, most such quarterly meetings would not have afforded the sacraments, even if the occasion was blessed, as this one was, with Anglican clergy. After 1784, the occasion did become *the sacramental* event in the life of Methodism.

The significance of Methodism's placement of the Eucharist in the quarterly meeting cannot be exaggerated. When in 1784, Methodism claimed ecclesial status for itself, it gave clearest statement in the Articles of Religion to what 'church' meant.[23] That statement, a classic Reformation conception of the church, was taken over from the Anglican Articles: "The visible Church of Christ is a congregation of faithful men in which the pure Word of God is preached, and the Sacraments duly administered according to Christ's ordinance, in all those things that of necessity are requisite to the same."[24] By that definition, Methodism came closest to being a visible church of Christ at quarterly meeting. There Methodism gathered those scattered around the circuit for the ordering of the church, the preaching of the word and the celebration of the sacraments. Another report, this one from 1787 and by Ezekiel Cooper, will illustrate.

> Love-feast began between eight and nine o'clock. We had the preaching-house well stowed with friends, and a glorious time we had. I don't know that ever I knew the people to get under a better way of speaking than they did to-day. The Lord's Supper was administered between ten and eleven o clock; then we went into the open woods to preach, got into a wagon, and then the speaker stood in a chair, so that we could both speak to and see the people. I preached the sermon from Acts xx, 31, 32. I had a field open to me, and both the people and myself were affected. The power of the Lord rested on us. I don't think I ever saw so large a congregation in the woods before behave so well; every one appeared to be still and attentive, an awe rested upon them, and I am persuaded that much good was done. Brothers Mills and Cromwell exhorted, and not in vain.[25]

This was not the 'church' that a traveler from Old England or New England might recognize—the typical parish encircled by its graveyard or a little community anchored to a green by meeting house. Instead, this congregation gathered at some appointed place, centered itself in the sharing of personal religious experiences that constituted love feast, reached out to ever larger circles through the preached word until it may have seemed that even the woods were taken in and then dispersed.

However strange it may seem, this four-times-a-year phenomenon might indeed be construed as the church of Methodism—that group of societies and classes that belonged to one another through a shared ministry, that in keeping with Methodist legislation exercised oversight of one another and of their resources, that experienced the full range of Methodist ritual offices only when together, that consequently on those occasions became a congregation where the word was preached and the sacraments administered, and that when so well constituted acted in mission to extend the promise of God's forgiveness to the world (the crowds) through a festival of preaching. The gathering seems to satisfy the criteria that early Methodists elaborated for 'church', but they seem not to have made the equation.

Another facet of conference they did recognize. When so gathered, Methodism not infrequently experienced revivals. That coincidence of quarterly meeting—indeed, of the several layers of conference—and revival is most dramatically evident in Lee's *Short History*. The narrative form of that work, as I noted at the outset, was that of successive conferences. Its substance, the substance of Methodist history, was revival. Lee's *Short History* is a history of Methodism as revival. Here, too, Lee established a standard long observed in the writing of Methodist history.

Here, too, Lee reflected a Methodist commonplace. Methodist preachers reported their work as successful revivals or as resistance to revival. Lee differed from both contemporaries and successors in recognizing the unity of form and substance, the relationship between the structure of Methodism and its mission, the coincidence of conference and revival.

Strikingly evident in Lee's telling is how frequently the revivals took place in conference—dramatic illustrations of which occurred in quarterly meetings of 1776, 1787, 1801, and 1802; in the annual conferences of 1788 and 1800; and in the General Conference of 1800.[26] So in Lee's account, the conference form of Methodism coincided with its revivalistic substance.[27] Conferences produced revivals; revivals took place in conference. Although Lee did not draw the conclusion that his argument suggests, by his precepts and those of eighteenth century Methodists generally he had proved conference to be an effective means of grace. For Methodists of that day believed that results gauged means. And what could be more a means of grace than what produced revivals? To this point we return below.

Here, a concluding paragraph or so about the multivalence of conference is in order. Lee never drew the theological implications of what he observed. Indeed, neither he nor his successor historians proved capable of making explicit and credible the multidimensionality and the richly religious texture of Methodism's conference structure, what in their universe of meaning might have been designated 'the gracious character of Methodist polity'. Instead, one dimension of conference—the political—gradually obscured its multifaceted force.

The political function of conference, though vital, was, as we have seen, only one of its several dimensions. Indeed, assent to conference's normative and constitutional prerogatives probably derived from conference's other competencies. It measured time and defined space. It established social boundaries, particularly among the preachers. It functioned politically, providing order and structure to the movement. Conference even gave, even if only implicitly, ecclesial expression to Methodism and fostered Methodist spirituality.

Other related dimensions might be explored. Conference had been a family of preachers headed and governed by John Wesley, and long remained a monastic-like order held together by affection, by common rules, by a shared mission, and by watchfulness of members over one another. It was a community of preachers whose commitment to the cause and one another competed with all other relationships. This brotherhood of religious aspiration was also known for its song. From the start, it functioned as a quasi-professional society concerned with the recep-

tion, training, credentialing, monitoring, and deployment of the preachers. This body would pool its resources to provide for the wants and needs
of its members, and when one of its members died, it was the agency of
memorial and memory. All of these impinged on conference's role as the
spiritual center of Methodism.[28] To spirituality I now turn.

Conference as a Means of Grace: British Roots

Methodist spirituality revolved around conference. Lee recognized this,
as we have seen. His contemporaries did as well. Casual notations in letters and journals indicate that revivals and conversions often occurred at
conference and conferences functioned to sustain and cultivate the religious life. Conference seemed to operate as a means of grace. It clearly
had what Methodists took to be the effects of grace.

Was this an American invention or did this pattern root in the Wesleyan
original? The answer is that both the multivalence of conference and its
intense spirituality were by design. Further, within Methodist thought and
legislation there were intimations of a theology of conference from which
much more might have been made.

To recognize the importance of conference to Methodist spirituality is
really to recall its centrality and multivalence. The entire system of Methodism, as John Lawson so aptly indicated, was means to a definite end, "a
way of life," "that a new awareness of God in Christ, and a new equipment
of moral power through the operation of the Holy Spirit, should come into
the lives of the people, to the renewal of Church and state."[29] All features
of Methodism oriented themselves toward that purpose, indeed, had been
adopted because they clearly served that purpose.

In the case of conference, its subservience to the redemptive purposes
of Methodism was implicitly recognized by Wesley and postulated in that
evolving document that assumed the place of constitution in Methodism,
"The Large Minutes." There Wesley recognized 'conference' as one of five
'instituted' means of grace. That designation and the character of the
other four—prayer, searching the Scriptures, the Lord's Supper, and fasting—suggest how very central to the Christian life and the Methodist
movement Wesley placed 'conference'.[30] The reference here was not specifically to the annual or to the quarterly Methodist meetings or conferences but rather to the mode of engagement, discipline, purpose, and
structure that they shared with all serious Christian encounter. By "Christian Conference" he meant a mode of conversation, oriented intentionally
and at every point to serve redemptive purposes.[31] So "Christian Confer-

ence" referred most properly to a Christian way of conducting human relationships. That general Christian walk or talk or way of being served, in this view, as a means of grace.[32]

Wesley seems not to have explicitly claimed that his conferences with preachers served as one of the instituted means of grace. He did not say, "Our annual gatherings partake of the more general endeavor that we call Christian Conference." Yet there are clear indications that they did. The very title of those encounters suggests that they belonged to that realm of Christian conversations. He called the record of those engagements, "Minutes of Some Late Conversations Between the Rev. Mr. Wesleys and Others."[33]

Even more suggestive of the idea that conference belonged to the category of means of grace were the expectations and rules enunciated for the conduct of conferences. These were to be spiritual and nurturing affairs. They were to be conducted as Christian conversations. A query put in 1747 clearly conveys this dimension of conference:

> Q. How may the time of this Conference be made more eminently a time of prayer, watching, and self-denial?
> A. 1. While we are in Conference, let us have an especial care to set God always before us. 2. In the intermediate hours, let us visit none but the sick, and spend all our time that remains in retirement. 3. Let us then give ourselves unto prayer for one another, and for the blessing of God on this our labour.[34]

During its meetings, then, conference concerned itself with the religious character of its proceedings. Conference's purposes reached beyond its own life and membership, as the second point in the preceding quotation indicates. While in session it also continued to oversee the spiritual well-being of the contiguous Methodist community and to reach out to the world. Often that involved services aimed at the Methodist people who would gather where conference met, a practice that the American conferences would continue.

Methodists sought to make conference a gracious affair by disciplining the conduct of proceedings. They also exercised a watch over individual members, particularly on entry but also in subsequent lifestyle. That oversight gave tone to the conference. Another query of the same year indicates how such expectations for conference as a whole connected with and expressed themselves in oversight of individual members.

> Q. Are our Assistants exemplary in their lives? Do we enquire enough into this?

A. Perhaps not. We should consider each of them who is with us a pupil
at the University, into whose behaviour and studies we should therefore
make a particular inquiry every day. Might we not particularly inquire,—
Do you rise at 4? Do you study in the method laid down at the last
Conference? Do you read the books we advise and no other? Do you see
the necessity of regularity in study? What are the chief temptations to
irregularity? Do you punctually observe the evening hour of retirement?
Are you exact in writing your journal? Do you fast on Friday? Do you
converse seriously, usefully, and closely? Do you pray before, and have
you a determinate end in, every conversation?[35]

Such oversight and such particularized expectations, familial, even paternal
in character, encouraged a deep spirituality in conference members. That
regimen was what gave the movement its name. It also produced a corporate
style, a conference culture, a conference of rigorous spirituality.

In time, such questions would become routinized and ritualized. Initially, they brought the preachers into deep engagement with Wesley and
one another. From that intimacy derived the bond of preacher to
preacher. From it proceeded also an intense corporate spirituality—akin
perhaps to modern encounter groups—which did permit conference to
function as a means of Methodist grace. Wesley caught the unitive and
spiritual (and familial/fraternal) expectations of conference in 1748:

Q. What can be done in order to [bring about] a closer union of our
Assistants with each other?
A. 1. Let them be deeply convinced of the want there is of it at present, and of the absolute necessity of it. 2. Let them pray that God
would give them earnestly to desire it; and then that He would fulfil
the desire He has given them.[36]

Thus the Wesleyan conference might appropriately be considered, in its
own terms, a means of grace. It was so by definition (if only implicitly). It
was so also by design and procedure, by expectation, by the rules and
regimen it set for itself, by the way it conducted its business. The conference operated with a clear sense of the redemptive activities which
should be carried out for the surrounding community and local Methodists. It exercised intense scrutiny and discipline over its members, pro-
ducing thereby great intimacy and a strong sense of unity. That body then
functioned with respect to its own membership and for Methodists generally as what Wesley intended as an instituted means of grace.

The implications were there to draw. Apparently Wesley did not draw
them and probably would not have wanted to, nor could he have afforded
to.[37] At any rate, Wesley's and Methodism's much-vaunted pragmatism—

the movement's willingness to adopt what would work without reflecting deeply on the whys and wherefores[38]—did not always serve it well in competitive situations and permits serious historical misunderstanding. By its action and by its structures Methodism committed itself to values, and one might even say, beliefs that it never brought fully into consciousness. In consequence, to understand Methodism's operative theology we really might well study what Methodism was and did and pay somewhat less attention to what it said. Its slighting the theological import of conference was, then, part of a more general pattern. Like its British counterpart, American Methodism failed to draw the implications of its practice. Its conferences sustained, perhaps even intensified, the British practices.

American Conferences as Means of Grace

The American conferences—quarterly and annual especially—resembled their British counterparts as means of grace.[39] The definition of conference American Methodists took straight from Wesley, incorporating "The Large Minutes" into the first *Discipline* of the new church with modest change. Wesley's paragraphs on "Instituted" means of grace came directly over into the new *Discipline*.[40] Accordingly, Americans employed the word "conference" to indicate "Christian conversation." For instance, the itinerant James Meacham frequently described the gatherings of ministers in both formal and informal meetings as "sweet Christian conference."[41] And American Methodists often drew attention to the way that conference nourished their religious life. Freeborn Garrettson, for instance, said of a 1777 conference, "I was greatly refreshed among the servants of God. . . . "[42] Martin Boehm felt that the Philadelphia Conference of 1808 was "like one great love-feast from beginning to end."[43] Yet true to form, the Americans shared Wesley's reluctance to capitalize on the definition of conference as a means of grace, recognize their own polity in that theological claim, and so elucidate the character of their quarterly, annual, and general conferences.

Nevertheless, design and procedure had their effects, notably the conversions described by Lee and others. To no small degree the conversion-producing character of the proceedings rested on the prominence given to the sharing of religious testimony, a witness that served its intended purpose of assuring the spiritual adequacy of members and candidates for the ministry but also stimulated the religious sensibilities of auditors and created a climate of heightened spirituality. The accounts of these proceedings provide us only hints of these dynamics.

The account of conference in 1792 by Stith Mead, Rehoboth, Green-brier District, is worth reproducing at some length. It shows how much the work of conference came to focus on the spirituality of its members.

Monday, 21st of May, 1792. We rode over Peter's Mountain by the Sweet Springs, to Brother Edward Keenan's at Rehoboth Chapel, Sinks of Greenbrier county, where I was glad to meet with the bishop, Rev. Francis Asbury; Hope Hull, Philip Cox, Jeremiah Abel, elders; Salathiel Weeks, John Lindsey, Bennett Maxey, and John Metcalf, deacons. John Kobler, remaining on trial, was received into connexion and ordained a deacon. James Ward and Stith Mead admitted on trial as probationers. Rev. Samuel Mitchell, local preacher, ordained deacon; Jeremiah Abel located. The above named preachers were all that composed and had business with the present Annual Conference. Bennett Maxey and John Kobler, by requests of the Bishop, related to the Conference their religious experience, and then the Conference adjourned until Tuesday at 8 o'clock, A.M., at which time J. Kobler, Geo. Martin, S. Mead were examined by the Bishop before the Conference, 1st, of our debts, 2dly, of our faith in Christ, 3dly, of our pursuits after holiness. The Bishop preached in the Chapel, which was near, at the usual hour, from Deut. v:27, "Go thou near, and hear all that the Lord our God shall say; and speak thou unto us all that the Lord our God shall speak unto thee, and we will hear it and do it." Brother Hope Hull preached from 1 Cor.i:23, "But we preach Christ crucified."

This afternoon I was requested by the Bishop to relate to the Conference my religious experience, which I accordingly did.

The appointments or stations were received from the Bishop this evening. . . .

Wednesday, 23rd. When met in Conference, we were all examined by the Bishop as to our Confession of Faith and orthodoxy of doctrine, agreeably to the economy of Wesleyan Methodism. . . . Bishop Asbury preached at the usual hour, Titus ii:1, "But speak thou the things which become sound doctrine." Rev. Hope Hull preached after the Bishop from 1 John iv:17, "Herein is our love made perfect, that we may have boldness in the day of Judgment, because as he is so are we in this world." A moving, melting time occurred during the sequel of this discourse; the holy Sacrament was administered; God manifested himself in his Spirit's power, the doors were opened, sinners came in, and there was a great shaking among the dry bones. Such a time, as I suppose, was never seen and experienced at this place before, ten souls were converted and many sinners cut to the heart. The lively exercises continued until near sundown.

Thursday, 24th. John Lindsey, Salathiel Weeks, and Bennett Maxey were ordained elders; John Kobler and Samuel Mitchell were ordained deacons. This is a rough, uncultivated country in soil, ways, and manners; the Conference was held in a log-body cabin-house, the residence of Brother G. Keenan, of Irish national descent. Our accommodation was the best in this part of the world.

The Conference broke about ten o'clock; we took leave of each other, and departed to our respective circuits.[44]

Striking in such accounts is the proportion of the conference devoted to the hearing of religious experience and to probing the spiritual condition of members. These were intensely introspective and communal affairs, punctuated by formal religious observances and by more routine business. Bishop Coke recognized the significance and power of such attention to spiritual autobiography in conference proceedings. He observed its value (and perhaps its institutionalization) in 1791 conferences:

> At each of our Conferences, before we parted, every Preacher gave an account of his experiences from the first strivings of the Spirit of God, as far as he could remember; and also of his call to preach, and the success the Lord had given to his Labours. It was quite new, but was made a blessing I am persuaded, to us all.[45]

What Coke meant by terming such procedure "quite new," is not clear. Perhaps he was struck with the prominence of spirituality in the conference life of American Methodism. In no small measure, the salience of spiritual concerns had to do with the relative youth of the conferences as organizations. As compared with the English and Irish Conferences that Coke knew so well, the American conferences were just taking shape, growing rapidly in size (and number), constantly recruiting new members and consequently devoting large proportions of their business to the rituals of admission—particularly testing the spiritual fitness of members. The chief business of conference seemed to be discerning spiritual gifts.

And the chief business of conference set the tone for conference. The sharing of testimony, the close attention to each other's spiritual journeys, created within conference a climate of piety. That process of discerning gifts, then, established the intense spirituality of these affairs—a spirituality which heightened intimacy, fraternity, unity and mission. The entire proceedings, the Methodist system as such, its structures of life and work functioned as what Methodists termed 'means of grace'.

This unity of structure and purpose, of form and substance, can be readily perceived in the early meetings of the Western Conference. The 1805 session evidenced a remarkable unity of spirituality and business.[46] That conference went deliberately about its business, hearing cases concerning slavery, caring for its temporal concerns, passing on a number of financial matters, attending to its own internal workings. It established two committees, "the 1st a Committee of Address, consisting of three members. 2nd, A Committee of Appropriations, consisting of four members.[47] Then the conference put the Committee of Address to heavy work, sending letters throughout the church: "to the several Quarterly Conferences," "to the several Annual Conferences," "to the Trustees of the Chartered Fund," "to the Brethren at Ebenezer," "to the absent members of the Conference," "to the General Book Stewards."[48] The Conference was deliberate about its business.

Such business, however, was enveloped by spirituality. The first day was devoted to the examination of elders and deacons in anticipation of their ordination. The conference also heard an address from Virginia, Baltimore, Philadelphia, New York, and New England conferences "which gave a summery statement of their temporal and spiritual concerns."[49] The following day, the conference ordered the writing of "an Epistle to the several Annual Conferences; Concerning the Temporal and Spiritual State of the Western Conference." It also minuted what appears to be a resolution of concern about the spiritual state of the world:

> It is the opinion of this Conference, that we live in an age in which there is great need to cry aloud, and spare not, and show lukewarm professors the danger of resting in a form only, and urge experimental and practical holiness, and teach sinners their utmost peril, and lead them to the Saviour of Men.[50]

The next day the conference undertook the examination of those admitted on trial. The minutes take special observance of their "profession of religion." The fourth day they devoted to sorting through the status of members. The next day they again endeavored to direct their spiritual resources to the wider Methodist community, resolving: "We have this day covenanted to pray for our brethren in the succeeding Conferences; especially in the time of their sitting."[51] That evening, in anticipation of the reading of appointments and separation the following day, "The Conference spent a few hours, this evening, in speaking of the work of God in their souls and Circuits."[52] By such procedures, the conference brought itself into being. The rules and regimen of Methodism produced a spiritual order.

The sharing of such testimony was the portal to the covenant that bonded preacher to preacher and preacher to church.[53] Out of that intensely intimate sharing was also born the deep sense of fellowship, spirituality, and unity that characterized the Methodist conference. That rich corporate interiority was often mentioned, even celebrated, but infrequently described. A rare glimpse comes in an account by Jesse Lee of his first conference, that of 1782 meeting at Ellis' Meeting House, Sussex.

The union and brotherly love which I saw among the preachers, exceeded every thing I had ever seen before, and caused me to wish that
I was worthy to have a place amongst them. When they took leave of
each other, I observed that they embraced each other in their arms,
and wept as though they never expected to meet again. Had the hea-
then been there, they might have well said, "See how these Christians
love one another!" By reason of what I saw and heard during the four
days that the Conference sat, I found my heart truly humbled in the
dust, and my desire greatly increased to love and serve God more
publically than I had ever done before.[54]

Lee caught the infectious quality, the power of such gatherings to elicit
religious experience. Expressions of commitment, intimacy, and unity stimulated the same in others. Expectations were unleashed that, in turn, other
conferences would have similar character. The 'gracious' dimension of these
occasions was a Methodist construction of reality, their acting and believing
that the religious life could and would be cultivated by these gatherings.

Also both that rich interiority and such powerful expectations easily
spilled into the wider life of Methodism. It is really no surprise that conferences proved to be scenes of revivals. Revivals came as the spiritual dynamisms of conference flowed into contiguous communities. As we have
already seen, these occurred frequently at the quarterly meetings, more
occasionally at annual conferences, and even at General Conference.[55]

Methodists knew that there was something eminently fitting about the
coincidence of revival with conference. They could not capture that ap-
propriateness in words, conceptually, theologically; eventually they did
find a pattern that allowed them to program for it. They called such programs camp meetings and scheduled them to coincide with quarterly
meetings and annual conferences. Thereby they institutionalized the revivalistic conference. Engineering served in the place of theory. That resulting unity between the conference and revival was a resounding
success. But camp meetings could not substitute for a theological understanding of conference or an adequate ecclesiology or a theology of the
church that made sense of actual Methodist workings.[56]

Camp meetings served to obscure the powerful, coherent but unarticulated ecclesiology in terms of which early Methodists labored. That ecclesiology found expression in their *Minutes*, diaries, journals, letters,
accounts of revivals, and even histories. Lee's *Short History*, in fact, portrayed the unity of form and substance, of conference and revival. Neither
he nor the church possessed the language to hold together what was experienced and described. And so ecclesiology became one thing, to be found
in the Articles of Religion. And polity another, to be encountered as con-

ference and understood from the *Discipline*. And revival yet a third, to be undertaken and appreciated as a distinct endeavor in its own right. And camp meetings a means to hold ecclesiology, polity, and revival together. Asbury perceived immediately that camp meetings must be promoted. At some level, he and his compatriots recognized that camp meetings were quintessentially Methodist. They were. Camp meetings served as a kind of unarticulated theology of salvation, a program that, in the absence of theory, held ecclesiology and polity and revival together. And camp meetings were a program that achieved what they promised. They were a means. So it was that camp meetings became Methodism's means of grace. So it was also that Methodists lost the intellectual opportunity to recognize conference as a means of grace.

Afterword

Methodists missed a theological, particularly an ecclesiological, opportunity. They lost an opportunity to construe their structures with the theological meanings and spiritual expectations that they in fact had implicitly carried. They let pass the opportunity to term conferences "means of grace," to reflect on the relation of form and substance, to grasp the nature and meaning of the new order of the church they had achieved in which a multivalent conference brought "church" into being around Word and Sacrament in a fashion that produced both order and revival.

At some level, Lee knew that the story of Methodism had to be set out in the form of conference and that its revivalistic substance took conference form. He did not have the words to conceptualize and pass on to future generations that relation of form and substance. So, he and his contemporaries watched as revival assumed its own form as camp and protracted meeting and conference transformed its spiritual substance into business. Those developments might not have been impeded by an adequate theory or theology of church order. And yet one cannot help but wish that at this as at other points, early Methodism had been more intellectually self-conscious.

At any rate, lacking an adequate ecclesial self-understanding, Methodists had difficulty with change. Lee would have drawn small comfort in the reassurance that the reduction of conference to polity and the displacement of revival by business were the costs of the institutionalization of charisma, or of growth, or of influence, or of development. With many Methodists he viewed the change as tragedy and would look back with great pathos on primitive Methodism.

What Lee might have told his compatriots was the following: The American conferences—quarterly and annual especially—resembled their British counterparts as means of grace. They were so by definition (if only implicitly), by design and procedure, by expectation, by the rules and regimen through which they operated, by the way they conducted business, by their clear sense of the redemptive activities which should be carried out for the surrounding community and local Methodists, by the intense scrutiny and discipline exercised over members, by the intimacy developed and by the unity achieved. In a very real sense conference functioned as a way of being the church. To understand early Methodist ecclesiology one has to look to that structure and the patterns associated with it. For conference was a means of grace.

6. The Four Languages of Early American Methodism

Tuesday, 23d. [Dec. 1794]. I rode to Mr. Laine's, in Littleborough, and at 2 o'clock, I preached on John xi.3. I had a crowded congregation, and the melting presence of God was amongst us. Many of the people could hardly refrain from weeping aloud. . . . Some of the people then went home, but soon returned. One man being in deep distress, began to cry aloud to God to have mercy upon his poor soul. . . . I talked, prayed, and sung, and while I was singing a visible alteration took place in his countenance, and I was inclined to think his soul was set at liberty. . . . I then took my text and preached on 1 Peter v.7. It was not long before another man was taken with a violent trembling, and crying, so that my voice was almost drowned. I was forced to stop. I then prayed for him, and he became more quiet. I then went on with my sermon. There was a great weeping in every part of the house. It appeared as if the whole neighbourhood was about to turn to God. I hope the fruit of this meeting will be seen after many days, and that the work of the Lord will revive from this time.[1]

Early Methodists were not afraid of the voice. Indeed, as this entry from Jesse Lee's journal indicates, theirs might be termed a movement of the voice—a preaching, singing, testifying, praying, shouting, crying, arguing movement. In Methodism, people found their voice. Methodists quite literally discovered ways of giving a voice—young men were pressed, one might even say in the military vernacular 'impressed', into preaching; hymn books virtually mandated congregational singing; love feasts made testifying into a quasi-sacrament; class meetings permitted the most outcaste of society to voice their inner concerns to God in the supporting presence of peers; shouting became a hallmark of Methodist utterance;[2] crying punctuated the discourse of both preacher and congregation; by arguing, Methodists stated and clarified their belief vis-à-vis prevalent, frequently Calvinist, options.[3] Methodists, then, were not afraid of the voice. When individual Methodists found theirs, they typically had a lot to say.[4] So they preached, sang, testified, prayed, shouted, cried, argued.

Their message may not have wrought a political revolution in the manner of the Puritan sermon.[5] It did produce quite remarkable conversions, built a mass movement, created a national church, and wrought a moral revolution. It produced effects that attest the cogency and power of the Methodist voice. A vignettee from 1790 records how loudly. Lee rode for a time with a man who had heard him preach but did not realize he rode with the preacher. "Ah! says he, these preachers speak louder than our ministers, and raise their heads, and spread their hands, and holler, as though they were going to frighten the people. I told him it would be well if they could frighten the people out of their sins."[6] Methodists did not, however, speak always with a single voice. And by the turn of the nineteenth century, the careful auditor might well have heard some discordance and detected that harmony was proving difficult to sustain. The difficulty would increase with time, for Methodists spoke to the new nation with not one but four voices, four languages, four formulations of doctrine.[7] Had the four languages been so recognized and identified, Methodists would have quickly protested that the four were but parts that made one whole. The truth is that Methodist reliance upon four distinguishable idioms proved both a source of great strength and surprising weakness.

The Four Languages

The four languages might be individually designated as (1) popular or evangelical; (2) Wesleyan; (3) episcopal or Anglican, and (4) republican. Each offered a surprisingly coherent and self-sufficient gospel. None was unique to American Methodism. Each was an ecumenical idiom. The unities produced by the four varied. Each pulled Methodists in a slightly different direction. (1) The popular language Methodists shared with all groups who made up the revival—those who spoke an evangelical or pietist tongue. With it, all the children of the awakenings could communicate. (2) The Wesleyan language defined the trans-Atlantic Methodist movement. Its terms denoted the particular features, practices, beliefs and rituals of Wesleyanism and bound Wesleyans together. (3) The episcopal language belonged to American Methodists because, with Wesley, they first claimed to be part of the Church of England and then in 1784 with Wesley's blessing became, in essence, a surrogate 'Anglican' church.[8] However, this particular affinity, between the Methodist Episcopal Church and the Protestant Episcopal Church, produced more conflict than unity. (4) The fourth language, the republican, defined the tradition of British political dissent, of Whiggery, and became an ideological feature of the American Revolution and a constitutive feature of American political consciousness.[9] By its use, Methodists proclaimed their patriotism and merged their voice with the other Protestant bodies that sought a national Christian unity for the new nation.

The four languages together shaped American Methodism. They seemed compatibile. Indeed, Methodists experienced them as constituting a unitary and unified discourse. They have apparently gone undifferentiated to this point. And yet from the earliest days they did pull the movement in different directions. They prove difficult to illustrate because they seldom occur close together (at least, until well into the nineteenth century). Several utterances from the year 1798 do show their nature and proximity to one another.[10] They also indicate the centripetal and centrifugal impulses of the four languages.

The Popular or Evangelical Language

The popular language, because it was common and a vernacular, is the least accessible today. It was the language of sermon, of class, of love feast, of camp meeting, of prayer. Such oral discourse often proves inaccessible to the historian. Fortunately, it was also the language of the journal. And there we can hear early Methodism and recover its popular voice. In the first citation from Lee, the reader has already met it. Another specifically from the year 1798 will recall its texture:

> Tuesday, 29th [May, 1798]. I rode to the Vansant's, at the head of Chester, and preached at 12 o'clock on Gal. vi. 7. *Be not deceived.* I had a very crowded house. I felt great liberty in preaching. The power and presence of the Lord was with us, and most of the people were in tears. Our hearts were closely united together, and I was much blessed amongst my old friends.[11]

In the journals, the Christian life was an affectionate and expressive affair. Preachers spoke with freedom; words uttered in great liberty produced tears; hearts were melted; souls found mercy and were closely knit in love; a new community of 'brothers' and 'sisters' defined itself over against the world and the distinctions of sex, class, position, and race that ruled therein; this new community reoriented itself toward Zion. Such terms recur throughout the journals, as this sampling of entries from Lee for 1794 should imply:

> I had life and liberty in preaching, and the people paid great attention.

> Sabbath I preached twice at Mr. Hutchen's, and the people were much melted under the word. I felt my soul much taken up with the things of God, and could truly say it was my meat and drink to do his blessed will. Then I went to N. Whiteirs' and met the class. The Lord was very precious to our souls and the people were much melted . . .

> Thursday, 27th. They collected the neighbours together, and at 11 o'clock I gave them a sermon, on Col. iii,14. It was a delightful season; my heart was humbled within me before God, and the people were melted into tears.

> I came to Mr. Bradford's at Farmington, and at 3 o'clock, I preached on John iv.14. Here the Lord was pleased to visit us again with his blessed presence. Tears flowed from many eyes, and it seemed to be a time of love.[12]

The terms with which Lee spoke (to himself as well as to the crowds) were richly biblical and doctrinally suggestive. They charted the Christian pilgrimage and the corporate life of the Christian community with words that all could understand. These terms comprise a surprisingly coherent religious world view, a popular evangelical or pietist world view. On Methodist tongues, they shaped themselves into Arminian tunes. But this language was not, for the most part, employed for formal doctrinal purposes.

The Wesleyan Language

For doctrine, Methodists invoked Wesley and drew upon a distinctly Wesleyan idiom. If in 1798 Lee epitomized Methodism's popular tongue, in 1798 John Dickins and Ezekiel Cooper epitomized the Wesleyan language. They were successive stewards of the Methodist Book Concern. The year 1798 saw both at this task as Dickins succumbed in that year to the yellow fever that struck Philadelphia.[13] It was the official and peculiar task of Dickins and then of Cooper to transmit the Wesleyan idiom. They did that through a rather remarkable series of publications, publications that sustained the remarkable publishing impulse of Wesley himself. So in 1798 Dickins saw that American Methodists had a *Pocket Hymn Book*, Wesley's *Explanatory Notes on the New Testament*, and *Sermons*, all three of which formally defined Methodist doctrine. Dickins published and/or carried other works of Wesley, volumes descriptive of the Christian life which Wesley had edited, the current *Discipline* which transmitted and recast Wesley's "The Large Minutes" for American usage, the *Minutes Taken at the Several Annual Conferences*—the record of the year's legislative gatherings—and *The Methodist Magazine*, 1798.[14] This literature prescribed an official Wesleyan language, one that the preachers had a stipulated duty to transmit. Their responsibilities included the charge, "To take care that every society be duly supplied with books."[15] With those books, Methodists spoke of classes, societies, circuits, quarterly meetings, annual conferences, stewards, local preachers, preachers, itinerancy, connection, discipline, love feasts, perfection, spirituous liquors, slavery, hymns, our sanctification, and the like.

Wesley had not intended that these terms define a self-sufficient religious system. He was adamant, in fact, that Methodism not separate itself from the Church of England. Yet British Methodism gravitated in that direction even during his life. And, of course, American Methodists with his blessing became an independent church. He made provision, when they did so, for the more distinctly ecclesial, sacramental, episcopal realities that he had always sought for Methodists through the established church. I turn to those provisions, that language, momentarily. Before doing so, I should observe that until 1784 American Methodists had really gotten along without the established church. Its clergy and parish churches did not dot the colonial landscape as they did the English countryside. A very few Anglican clergy cooperated with the American Methodists. And so American Methodists were tempted from the very start to regard this Wesleyan language as self-sufficient. After Wesley's death, British Wesleyanism did. American Methodism came very close to the same policy in 1779 in the Fluvanna division, when for a time it seemed that the southern half of the movement would proceed with the resources at hand to establish a church and did in fact ordain and celebrate the sacraments. The northern half of the movement followed the leadership of Asbury, respected Wesley's desire that Methodism remain within the Anglican Church, dis-fellowshiped those who had struck for independence, and awaited a dispensation from Wesley. The southern group capitulated to Asbury, but the possibility it represented, of regarding the distinctly Wesleyan idiom as a self-sufficient religious system, would remain a Methodist temptation. American Methodists would be tugged by it every time they sought to converse with their British counterparts. That conversation, in particular, required such Wesleyan terms.

The Episcopal Language

In the same year of 1798, the episcopal language was clearly stated in a volume that was "sold by John Dickins." That year *The Doctrines and Discipline of the Methodist Episcopal Church in America* carried a striking subtitle: "With Explanatory Notes by Thomas Coke and Francis Asbury." The two bishops undertook a rather revealing, and, one should add, rare exercise of the teaching office. By their annotations, undertaken at the behest of the prior General Conference, they explained and defended Methodism's episcopal claims. They did so, at least in part, to answer the criticisms levied by James O'Kelly and to staunch the hemorrhaging loss of good Methodists to his protest schism.[16]

O'Kelly had challenged the episcopacy and its power, politically by moving that preachers injured by episcopal appointment have a right of appeal to the conference and rhetorically by inveighing against episcopal tyranny. Answering that latter charge proved to be a major thrust of the bishops' commentary. The first section of the *Discipline*, "Of the Origin of the Methodist Episcopal Church," lent itself to a disquisition, three times as long as the section, defending Methodism's adoption of episcopal government, explaining the nature of Wesley's own episcopal authority, repudiating the conception of *"an apostolic, uninterrupted succession,"*[17] and adducing the New Testament texts supportive of an episcopal plan. In the second section, "Articles of Religion," the bishops likewise marshalled the New Testament support for these Anglican affirmations.

The *Discipline* did not include, and so no annotations were given to, the text of the eucharistic rite or baptism. However, the comments on the specific articles devoted to the sacraments, "Of the Sacraments," "Of Baptism," "Of the Lord's Supper," and "Of both Kinds," sections XVI to XIX, clearly called to mind that aspect of Methodism's Anglican character. Short, later sections of the *Discipline*, "Of Baptism" and "Of the Lord's Supper," would have had some of the same force.[18]

In the sacraments, in the Articles and in its episcopal government (bishop, elder, deacon), Methodists applied to themselves the terminology of Anglicanism. Theirs was not a high church language after the fashion of Archbishop Laud, the Non-Jurors, the early Wesley, or the nineteenth-century Tractarians. It was rather an Anglican terminology familiar to Americans who had known the established church in the colonies.[19] When it talked about its government, when it celebrated the sacraments, when it identified the core of its belief, and when it ordained ministers, Methodism spoke an episcopal tongue.

To be sure, Methodists understood that tongue to be an episcopal *Methodism*. The annotated *Discipline* clearly made that point. It did so by its very appearance, through the text, and in explicit commentary. The Wesleyan language and that of Anglicanism were put together. The page and a half which constituted section IV, "Of the Election and Consecration of Bishops, and of their Duty," insisted, for instance, that American Methodism's episcopacy simply gave suitable ecclesial expression to Wesley's style of leadership. We "must observe," stated the bishops, "that nothing has been introduced into Methodism by the present episcopal form of government, which was not before fully exercised by Mr. Wesley."[20] Elsewhere the notes commented on features of Methodism that rooted in the Wesleyan movement and explained distinctive practices and structures. In that sense and as should be expected, the volume transmitted the Wesleyan language as well as the episcopal. The notes functioned—particularly through the common appeal to the New Testament and the practice of the primitive church—to cement the bond of Methodist and Episcopal idioms and warrant the church's name and self-understanding. And yet the bond was not always a firm or a happy one.

The Republican Language

In the year 1798, James O'Kelly epitomized the unhappiness over the episcopal character of Methodism. One of the eminent leaders of early Methodism, O'Kelly sought directions for the movement that threw him into conflict with Asbury and Coke. He criticized Asbury's experiment with a council, prompted the creation of the general conference, and at the first such, the General Conference of 1792, initiated a frontal challenge to episcopal power. He proposed, by motion, that preachers have the right to appeal to the conference the appointment made for them by the bishop. The motion eventually failed and O'Kelly walked out to form the Republican Methodist Church.[21]

It has been easy for Methodists to dismiss O'Kelly but, in fact, he spoke for many early Methodists. His cause had considerably more appeal than the numbers which rallied to his banner would suggest.[22] In 1798, O'Kelly produced *The Author's Apology for Protesting Against the Methodist Episcopal Government*.[23] A few citations will illustrate his appeal and the language that sustained it:

> If Christians are free citizens of Zion, they should prize those liberties, seeing they were purchased with the precious blood of Christ.

Thomas and Francis were our Superintendents, as Presiding Elders, according to John's appointment. But they were not elected by the suffrage of conference, although it is so written in the book of discipline.

Ah, Francis was born and nurtured in the land of kings and bishops, and that which is bred in the bone, is hard to be got out of the flesh.

O Heavens! Are we not Americans! Did not our fathers bleed to free their sons from the British yoke? And shall we be slaves to ecclesiastical oppression?[24]

This was republican language, the rhetoric of the British Commonwealthman tradition, the world view of radical Whiggery, the ideology of the American Revolution.[25] It described a world in which republics were rare and fragile institutions, where power ever threatened the liberties of the people, where authority transmuted itself into tyranny unless checked and vigilantly watched, where freedom's only hope lay in the collective resolve of a virtuous citizenry, where virtue easily succumbed to luxury or the inducements of power, where the fate of the republic therefore rested with the virtue or corruption of its citizens. Its recurrent terms were virtue, liberty, corruption, tyranny, republic, rights, and reason.

Here, as in the case of the other three languages, we find a coherent world view. Republicanism offered Methodism a richly elaborated mythology that clearly beckoned O'Kelly—a saga which fit the present into a history of republics and of tyranny. To employ it was to adopt a historical account that situated today's perils in a narrative that recalled Israel's political experience, the republics of Greece, the Norman Yoke, the Glorious Revolution, and now the American Revolution. O'Kelly effectively claimed that mythology and conjured up its visions of tyranny and corruption.

O'Kelly also strove to claim that mythology for Christian ends. He did so clumsily, proclaiming Christians "free citizens of Zion," glossing the distinction between church and state, and construing Asbury as tyrant. The generality of Methodists thought that he protested too much. It is perhaps useful to distinguish his rhetorical maneuver from its political objectives. He was struggling to bring together Christian theology and the ideology of the Revolution. He wanted Methodism to make sense in relation to its political context. He reached for a public theology. In that, he was a Methodist and southern participant in an enterprise largely dominated by Calvinists and New Englanders. This national period was a time when other Protestants, particularly those from the Reformed camp, were struggling toward a theology that would embrace the new republic in the larger cause of God's redemption of the world. Behind their efforts lay a century and a half of colonial experience with a godly state and, of course, the challenges to establishments stimulated by the Revolution and new constitution making. Intent on sustaining that Godly civic order despite disestablishment, Reformed theocrats fought for their own vision of the new order of the ages, fearing on the one side the popular threats represented by the O'Kellys who embraced what seemed to them disorder in Christian and republican language and, on the other side, the elite like Jefferson who seemingly would sacrifice Christianity to the self-evident truths of enlightenment. Reformed theologians construed these and other challenges to Christian order as conspiracies. Conspiratorial visions made sense of the pell-mell of post-revolutionary America.[26] In the year that O'Kelly wrote, eminent New England divines uncovered an international conspiracy that conveniently linked various enemies of the Puritan way with Jeffersonians, the zealots of the French Revolution, Bavarian Illuminati, and the Anti-Christ.[27] The new republic, they thought, was at risk. Eventually the crisis passed and Presbyterians and Congregationalists reworked this strident millennialism into a theology of the nation. This public theology combined republicanism with Christian and particularly Calvinist notions of order in ways that would shape both the national political culture and Protestant denominations. Under its banner, they labored for a Christian America.[28]

With these Reformed contemporaries, O'Kelly shared little more than a fear of conspiracy. His theology was Arminian not Calvinist, his political rhetoric Jeffersonian not Federalist, and his religious policy separationist not integral. Yet his rhetorical maneuver was one that would ultimately come to serve those Reformed purposes. They, like he, would eventually baptize republicanism. In that sense, O'Kelly's protest and his critique belonged to this larger effort to adapt the ideology of the Revolution to Christian use and to give Christian direction to the nation.

O'Kelly's adoption of republicanism probably produced greater resonances within Methodism than his treatment by Methodist historians would suggest. Certainly Asbury and the leadership loyal to him experienced O'Kelly as a formidable threat. And the threat he posed was at a point of great vulnerability. Its linguistic structure was fluid and ill defined, its values unguarded and open to divergent interpretation, its several languages beckoning the movement in different directions. By appealing to this powerful democratic idiom, O'Kelly invoked Methodism's own sense of conspiracy and resort to order. In the trench warfare that followed, O'Kelly lost the allegiance of many who had initially rallied to his banner. But over the long haul O'Kelly's cause, if not his movement, would prosper. O'Kelly laid claim to a republican language that would increasingly become the Protestant idiom and eventually also the Methodism idiom. It gave shape to the reform impulse of the 1820s that resulted in the Methodist Protestant Church. It also found its way into mainstream episcopal Methodism. That appropriation is illustrated in the historical narratives of Nathan Bangs and his successors. They wove the American republic into the fabric of Methodist history. They also wove it into Methodist life.[29] By mid-century, the northern church would become as zealous for Christian republicanism as any of the Reformed.

Babel or Pentecost?

Methodists found the four languages useful. They did not, in the manner of Calvinists or Lutherans, strive to bring the four languages into a common systematic framework. Rather they employed them as occasion demanded. At times, more than one seemed appropriate, so they juxtaposed them. Annual conferences frequently demanded several languages. The *Minutes* document the ease with which Methodists negotiated the several languages, moved between them, employed them successively. Those for 1798, for instance, reported the traditional Wesleyan questions in terms of which the church ordered itself:

Quest. 1.   Who are admitted on trial?
Quest. 2.   Who remain on trial?
Quest. 3.   Who are admitted into full connexion?
Quest. 7.   Who are under a location . . . ?
Quest. 8.   Who are the supernumeraries?
Quest. 9.   What Preachers, have withdrawn themselves from our Order and Connexion?
Quest. 10. Who have been expelled from our order and connexion?
Quest. 12. Are all the Preachers blameless in life and conversation?
Quest. 13. What numbers are in Society?
Quest. 14. Where are the Preachers stationed this year?
Quest. 15. When and where shall our next conferences be held?[30]

The *Minutes* also framed questions in episcopal terms:

Quest. 4.   Who are the Deacons?
Quest. 5.   Who are the Elders?
Quest. 6.   Who have been elected by the unanimous suffrages of the General Conferences, to superintend the Methodist Episcopal Church in America?[31]

The Episcopal and Wesleyan terms, questions, and processes were juxta-posed but not really conceptually unified.[32]

Also in the *Minutes* appeared a question that elicited responses in the popular idiom. Question 11 read "Who have died this year?" The entry for John Dickins recounted his considerable services to the Methodist cause and proclaimed that "His works shall praise him in the gates of Zion." An entry for James King invoked popular images, but also entered a republican note: "He was about 24 or 25 years of age.—He gave his life, his labours, and his fortune to the Church of Christ and his brethren; and was a friend to religion and liberty."[33]

Less formal accounts of conference also juxtaposed popular, Wesleyan, and episcopal motifs. Jesse Lee reported on a 1798 conference. In his rendering, the tremendous power unleashed by the Methodist movement clearly presupposes and requires three of the several languages. The Wesleyan occasion—conference—and the episcopal rituals—ordination and eucharist—unleashed a revival that Lee could only convey with popular language.

> Wednesday, 29th [August 1798], conference began in Readfield; we were closely engaged all day; the next day we set in conference very early, and broke up at 8 o'clock. At 9, we held lovefeast, and had a large number of Methodists together, and none else. They spoke freely, and feelingly. It was a good time. At 11 o'clock Mr. Asbury preached a good sermon. . . . Then we ordained Timothy Merritt, Robert Yellaley, and Aaron Humphrey, deacons, and Roger Searle, an elder. It was a very solemn time at the ordination; but the people were so crowded in the gallerys that were not finished, that some of the joists gave way, and frightened the people very much for a few minutes, and some were slightly hurt. Then I preached on Rom. xvi.20. My soul was much animated with the presence of the Lord. The people were melted into tears. It was a precious time to many. Then we administered the Lord's Supper. I suppose there were above two hundred communicants; it was a most solemn time at the table.[34]

In Lee's account as in the official *Minutes*, the three languages function together. But did they, do they, really cohere?

Four Distinct Languages and Literatures?

At various points this volume has suggested that Methodists adopted and used the languages without clarifying their relationships and compatibility. This point has been made frequently with respect to the Wesleyan and episcopal idioms and often illustrated with the confusion over ministry occasioned by the two sets of terms and processes by which and through which ministry was and is conceived.[35] Candidates proceeded along two tracks into Methodist ministry, one culminating in conference membership, the other in elder's orders.

This essay extends that point to the two other Methodist languages. Each of their central concerns has been illustrated. It is worth underscoring here what has been implicitly documented, namely that they differed sufficiently to generate separate literatures. The popular language produced journals and diaries. To it also belonged firsthand accounts of revivals and conversions, which in evangelical literature became a distinct genre of literature, "religious intelligence" or "missionary intelligence." Obituaries and correspondence frequently invoked popular terms as well. These items found space in *The Christian Advocate* and other 'popular' literature. Popular literature stemmed from and expressed Wesley's own example, command, and instruction. Such colloquial expressiveness attested Wesley's sense of the value of testimony. Recognizing a distinctive Wesleyan literature and language should not underestimate Wesley's own role in their popular counterparts.

Still, one can recognize a semiseparate Wesleyan literature. Wesley generated, and American Methodism continued to print and transmit, an array of publications designed to sustain Wesleyan practice and institutions. The Wesleyan literary standards were *Minutes, Discipline*, hymnbooks, Wesley's own *Works*, the normative *Sermons,* and *Notes on the New Testament*, and eventually successful magazines. This Wesleyan literature—really a Wesleyan literary revolution—fueled Methodist expansion.[36] By this grammar, the movement distinguished itself and sold its wares in the free enterprise of American Protestantism.

Methodists generated 'episcopal' literature for doctrinal, liturgical, and apologetical purposes—when formal self-expression was required. The first such instance was Bishop Coke's sermon at the 1784 organizing conference.[37] Among the most powerful was his episcopal colleague's 1813 Valedictory Address.[38] Apologetics produced the greatest volume. Attacked by Episcopalians and Calvinists, Methodists responded in episcopal mode. Among early spokespersons were Martin Ruter, Nathan Bangs, John Emory, and Wilbur Fisk.[39]

Within episcopal Methodism, O'Kelly's example and publications received only scorn. His production discouraged Methodist republicanism for at least a generation. Still, there were other early anticipations of Methodism's later republican output. Notable were the formal declarations of "General Fast" and "General Thanksgiving" that the church issued in 1795.[40] Republican items appeared in significant number in the succession of Methodist reform movements. The Methodist Protestants, for instance, essentially recast Methodism into a republican mode. So also did northern episcopal Methodism as it thought about the place of the church in American society. That redefinition of the mission of the movement can be readily discerned in the succession of mid-century histories of Methodism. The Civil War accented the tendency to give republican meaning to Methodism (to be sure only on the northern side). By that point, this language too had achieved full normative status within the movement.

Four Doctrines?

More significant, and troubling to Methodism, than separate literatures were the doctrinal tensions between and among the languages. It would stretch their differences to speak of separate doctrines. Methodists, after all, experienced them as compatible. The languages did, however, pull in different directions. They gave distinct answers to the fundamental questions which Methodism, with Wesley, took as its theological agenda:

1. What to teach;
2. How to teach; and,
3. What to do; that is how to regulate our doctrine, discipline, and practice.[41]

Each, for instance, offered a distinct notion of what it meant to be a church. The definition most likely to come to mind was and is an episcopal one, formally rendered in the Articles and evoked in the liturgy:

> XIII. Of the Church
>
> The visible Church of Christ is a congregation of faithful men, in which the word of God is preached, and the sacraments duly administered according to Christ's ordinance, in all those things that of necessity are requisite to the same.[42]

Whether early American Methodists regarded this episcopal—really Reformation—definition as adequate to their connectional and missionary sense of the church we do not fully know.

We have seen that when they spoke in popular terms about themselves, when they talked about Methodism as an ecclesial reality, they reached for a very different image. The term most frequently employed—the popular conception—was biblical. Methodists spoke of Zion, a term that evoked both historical Israel and the eschatological New Jerusalem. Asbury, for instance, rode into North Carolina in 1795 and observed:

> This country improves in cultivation, wickedness, mills, and stills; a *prophet of strong drink* would be acceptable to many of these people. I believe that the Methodist preachers keep clear, both by precept and example; would to God the members did so too! Lord, have pity on weeping, bleeding Zion![43]

This popular notion lacks the formality and precision of the episcopal definition. It had compensating strengths for Methodism. It located Methodism in the economy of salvation, both historically and eschatologically. It identified Methodism with the people of God, the corporate, trans-congregational reality of God's chosen ones. It legitimated a dynamic, political self-understanding and orientation to the world.

The Wesleyan contribution to ecclesiology—conference—lacks Zion's connection to salvation history. Nor was it or is it frequently given doctrinal status. However, in conference and particularly in the quarterly conference or quarterly meeting, Methodists gave vivid expression to how they thought the people of God should live and what it meant to offer grace to lost sinners.[44] Quarterly meetings dramatized Methodism's missionary conception of the church and of the gospel. Lee's report, cited above, captured the ecclesial drama. Methodism treated conference as an ecclesial reality, even if lacking the explicit historical and eschatological referent of Zion and the formal precision of the episcopal definition. Conference and quarterly meetings made up in act what they lacked in form. They satisfied the episcopal definition with explosive eucharists and met the popular eschatological hope by revival.

The republican ecclesiology focused on the nation. A Christian republic, God's New Israel, a redeemer nation, a Christian America—the terms for it are various. Early Methodists gave somewhat hesitant and tentative assent to this Calvinist doctrine.[45] Their commitment to it gradually increased so that by midcentury at least the northern Methodists had made it constitutive of their self-understanding. They came to believe in "the Nation with the Soul of a Church."[46] They viewed themselves as a national church, sometimes even *the* national church. The function of this conception was similar to Zion. Belief in a Christian America, in fact, represented the working out of a biblical, indeed Hebraic and covenantal political theology. It proved to be a compelling and powerful vision of Christian community, one that dominated American Protestantism and American society well into the twentieth century. This is not the place to offer a sustained criticism of that vision. Suffice it to say that it lured Methodists into politicizing their ecclesiology, giving their missionary sense of the church a rather limited societal referrent, and fixing their purposes in national not global terms.

Implications

The different ecclesiologies offered distinct hopes, functioned with distinct notions of what constituted authority,[47] identified distinct purposes for corporate Christian life, and conceived the unity of the church in distinct fashion. The four languages produced theological multiplicity on other doctrines as well, particularly in such areas as anthropology, soteriology, and ethics. The languages functioned, then, to offer Methodists a range of theological options, various identities, and choices as to what constituted Methodism. They did so when each generated a distinct theological option, as with ecclesiology; they did so even more frequently in combinations. For the most part, however, Methodism managed to hold together and live with its four languages.

Its failures at unity had something to do with language. The different possible Methodist identities and the linguistic cacophony partially explain later fissures in the Methodist movement. There is a rough correspondence, for instance, between republicanism and the Methodist Protestant Church; between popular concerns of early Methodism and both Black Methodism and the Holiness movement; between episcopal emphases and the Methodist Episcopal Church, South; and between Wesleyan self-understandings and the Methodist Episcopal Church. It is instructive, for instance, that one of the African American Methodisms chose to imbed Zion in its name. Nevertheless, these correspondences are only rough. Each movement typically drew on all four languages. The African Methodist Episcopal Zion Church, for instance, scrupulously maintained Wesleyan patterns and episcopal practices; in its pursuit of abolition, it also found republican values important. Still, the vitalities of popular Methodism were what made African Methodism attractive to Black Americans.

If we do not find various Methodisms breaking cleanly along these linguistic lines, we might profitably understand their peculiar appeal and dynamic by studying the internal configurations and relative priority each gave these languages.

Similarly, the debates and disputes within each movement become more intelligible when Methodism's several frames of reference are taken seriously and the consequent divergences of value and of commitment respected for what they are. Because of their plural languages, Methodists frequently talked past one another.

The problem for the historian is to make some sense of a Methodist past characterized by this complex interplay of languages. The interpreter may, at times, be tempted by the impulse (to which the movement or portions thereof occasionally succumbed) to take one of these languages as authentic, or controlling, or basic, and to construe Methodism in its terms alone. That lure has shaped histories as well as policy. Methodism is better understood by recognizing the place and power of all the languages. The four languages, after all, have been claimed, used, valued, and even championed. They represent for the historian rich intellectual resources, symbol systems in terms of which to understand the movement. The question raised but not answered by this volume is the relation these languages have had to one another. Was it Babel or Pentecost?

Appendix
The Joint Commission on
the Origin of American Methodism

Chapter 4 alludes to an official enquiry into Methodist origins, one jointly undertaken by the northern and southern churches (and the Methodist Protestants), which issued a formal finding on behalf of southern origins. That triumph for the southern view occurred in the following fashion.

In 1912, J. F. Goucher presented a memorial on behalf of the Baltimore Conference to the General Conference of The Methodist Episcopal Church, "proposing an inquiry into the origin of American Methodism and providing for the sesquicentennial of American Methodism" (*Journal of the Twenty-Sixth Delegated General Conference of the Methodist Episcopal Church*, 1912, 277). The Committee on Itinerancy, to which the memorial was referred, proposed:

> WHEREAS, The time and place of the origin of American Methodism is in dispute, as between Sam's
> Creek, Maryland,
> and New York City; and,
> WHEREAS, The sesquicentennial of that event is approaching; therefore,
>
> *Resolved*, . . . That the General Conference appoint a Commission of seven members, at least three of whom shall come from the vicinity of New York, and three from the vicinity of Baltimore, and one at large, who, together with similar Commissions from the Methodist Episcopal Church, South, and the Methodist Protestant Church (if such be appointed), shall inquire carefully into and, if possible, determine whether the priority belongs to Maryland or to New York. (Ibid., pp. 591–92. A second resolution called for "the proper observance of this greatest event in the religious life of the Republic.)

Four years later, in 1916, a Joint Commission on the Origin of American Methodism reported back to the General Conference on "the question of *Priority* as between Philip Embury and Robert Strawbridge—New York and Maryland." The report indicated that by personal request and published notice, the Commission had solicited evidence and argument. Some "*two hundred* volumes, typewritten papers and manuscripts" had been submitted. Though without two members who had declined to participate, a quorum from the three churches had examined and discussed the evidence. By written ballot, the Commission voted 14 to 0 in favor of Robert Strawbridge's priority. "The Joint Commission then proceeded to vote separately upon various historic facts," unanimously determining the following:

99

1. That Philip Embury began to preach and formed a Society in the City of New York, some time during the year 1766.
2. That Robert Strawbridge came to Maryland and settled on Sam's Creek, Frederick County, about 1761.
3. That Mr. Strawbridge began to preach as soon thereafter as he had "arranged" his home.
4. That Mr. Strawbridge baptized Henry Maynard as early as 1762 or 1763.
5. That John Evans was converted as early as 1763 or 1764.
6. That Mr. Strawbridge began forming societies as early as 1763 or 1764.
7. That among all those who have wrought constructively in the development of Methodism in America, to the work of Robert Strawbridge in Maryland belongs the distinction of priority. (*Journal of the Twenty-Seventh Delegated General Conference the Methodist Episcopal Church*, 1916, 1503–1505)

Should the august forum of General Conference, the exacting scholarly procedures, and a balloted conclusion not assure the finality of Baltimore's claims, the commission submitted a report of 116 pages summarizing the evidence and sustaining its conclusion (*The Origin of Methodism in America*).

A minority of two, representing New York, nevertheless protested these findings. They screamed foul. Unwilling to let the matter rest with a formal report, they, like the majority, buttressed their report with a small book, also of about 100 pages. H. K. Carroll's title stated the matter grimly: *The First Methodist Society in America. When and Where Was it Formed? By Embury or Strawbridge?* In report and book, he argued that the case remained open and the majority's decision was a sham. The Joint Commission, Carroll inferred, had been stacked. Ten of its fourteen members came from Baltimore. Most of them, alleged Carroll, had "participated in a celebration in the fall of 1914, at Sam's Creek, of what was called the sesquicentennial of the beginning of Methodism in America" (9). The members of the Joint Commission, then, had voted by ritual act before they had looked at the evidence. The minority report further pointed out the obvious. No New York representative had participated. Why? The New Yorkers had absented themselves in deference to episcopal recommendation that action be delayed. Also, in the spirit of the originating MEC resolution, MEC commissioners should have reached their own conclusions before meeting with representatives of the other two churches. Thus the conclusions, they asserted, "seem to us quite inconclusive." The definiteness of Embury's claims should be preferred to the indefiniteness of Strawbridge's.

> For these and other reasons we earnestly recommend that the whole matter be committed to an impartial committee, to be nominated by the American Historical Association, and appointed by our Bishops, which Committee shall include one or two members of the legal profession, the hearings of this Committee to be conducted with open doors and its decision to be final. (*Journal*, 1916, 1505–1507)

The irony here is delightful—southern Methodists (traditionally committed to a strong episcopacy and wary of the more democratic power of General Conference) resolving historical issues by the democratic process and the northerners (characteristically wary of episcopacy and committed to a strong General Conference) appealing desperately to highest authority—the AHA, the ABA, the episcopacy.

For further discussion of the matter of southern or northern origins and the real import thereof, see chapter 4.

Notes

Introduction

1. William H. Williams employs this phrase as the title of his fine volume, *The Garden of Methodism: The Delmarva Peninsula, 1769–1820* (Wilmington: Del.: Scholarly Resources, 1984), a work very congenial to this endeavor and referred to at several points.

2. See *The Experience and Travels of Mr. Freeborn Garrettson* (Philadelphia: Parry Hall, 1791). Also reprinted in *American Methodist Pioneer, The Life and Journals of The Rev. Freeborn Garrettson, 1752–1827*, ed. Robert Drew Simpson (Rutland, Vt.: Academy Books, 1984), 35–144. Both his published *Experience and Travels* and the more extensive mss. version of his journals document Garrettson's and Methodism's troubles in Eden. They evidence the life-threatening conflict into which the radical antislavery, frequently pacifist Gospel threw Methodist preachers and also show that the Tory sympathies of a few Methodist preachers and the anti-independence stance of Mr. Wesley exposed the whole movement to suppression.

3. This is a concern in most Methodist histories. Special attention to it is given by Frank Baker, "The Americanization of Methodism," *Reflections upon Methodism during the American Bicentennial*, ed. Richard Heitzenrater (Dallas: Bridwell Library, 1985), 3–20; Douglas R. Chandler, "Towards the Americanizing of Methodism," *Methodist History*, 13 (Oct. 1974), 3–16; Theodore C. Linn, "Religion and Nationalism: American Methodism and the New Nation in the Early National Period, 1766–1844" (Ph.D. diss., Drew University, 1971); and John Abernathy Smith, "How Methodism Became a National Church in the United States," *Methodist History*, 20 (Oct. 1981), 13–28.

4. Nathan O. Hatch, *The Democratization of American Christianity* (New Haven and London: Yale University Press, 1989). Hatch dwells on the ironies mentioned here (as well as others) but accents them differently.

5. For a careful discussion of the problems in explanations predicated upon sect-to-denomination development, see William H. Swatos, Jr., "Beyond Denominationalism: Community and Culture in American Religion," *Journal for the Scientific Study of Religion*, 20 (Sept. 1981), 217–27, and Alan W. Eister, "H. Richard Niebuhr and the Paradox of Religious Organization: A Radical Critique," in *Beyond the Classics?*, ed. Charles Y. Glock and Phillip E. Hammond (New York: Harper & Row, Publishers, 1973), 355–408.

6. An alternative biblical construction of the plurality of languages is, of course, Pentecost. Both images yield appropriate insight. Early Methodism was indeed a Pentecost, in which the Spirit rained and during which the variety of tongues gave testimony to the rich possibilities ahead. The stories of Methodist growth and prosperity constitute an appropriate extrapolation of that image. But, as this volume also endeavors to show, Methodism also had its spiritually darker side. The confusion of tongues also had its negative side. And 'babel' extrapolates that image.

101

7. Such language does recur through Methodist journals. See, for instance, *American Methodist Pioneer;* John McLean, *Sketch of Rev. Philip Gatch* (Cincinnati: Swormstedt & Poe, 1854); or the documents in William Warren Sweet, *Religion on the American Frontier, 1783–1840,* 4 vols. (New York: Cooper Square Publishers, 1964; first published by University of Chicago Press, 1946); IV, *The Methodists.*

8. It came closest to canonical status in Methodism's hymnody which spoke in these terms. Charles Wesley's hymns, in particular, integrated Wesleyan and Pietist concerns with those of Protestant orthodoxy. Methodists have often remarked, typically in retrospect, that hymnody served as Methodism's teaching office, instructing the people in Methodist theology. Unfortunately, Methodism did not really grant the hymnbook such a status. It did not privilege its hymnbook in the way that it did the Articles of Religion, Wesley's *Sermons,* and his *Notes on the New Testament.* So while its use came close to being mandatory, the hymnbook did not achieve canonical status. On the "Restrictive Rules" and Methodist doctrine, see Thomas C. Oden, *Doctrinal Standards in the Wesleyan Tradition* (Grand Rapids: Francis Asbury Press of Zondervan Publishing House, 1988).

9. For a superb reading of this second language's ability to carry the freight of Methodist meaning, see Robert E. Cushman, *John Wesley's Experimental Divinity: Studies in Methodist Doctrinal Standards* (Nashville: Kingswood Books/ Abingdon Press, 1989).

10. And one could argue that down to the late twentieth century, American Methodists have struggled to hold together these two springs of their identity— one that stems from the dynamisms of evangelical life and from the Wesleyan channeling thereof and another that has its source in the formal, theological literature of the Anglican Reformation.

11. The first and last two essays examine the interplay of and tensions among these first three languages.

12. The literature on public or civil religion is vast. Among the most perceptive treatments are John F. Wilson, *Public Religion in American Culture* (Philadelphia: Temple University Press, 1979) and Donald G. Jones, "Civil and Public Religion," *Encyclopedia of the American Religious Experience,* ed. Charles H. Lippy and Peter W. Williams, 3 vols. (New York: Charles Scribner's Sons, 1988), III, 1393–1408.

13. Here this account does diverge somewhat from Nathan Hatch's reading. It suggests that it is less the language of the Revolution, less the republican idiom, than that of the Pietist and Wesleyan vernacular which gave Methodism its popular character.

1. Community, Fraternity, and Order

1. *The Journal and Letters of Francis Asbury,* 3 vols., ed. Elmer T. Clark et al., (Nashville: Abingdon Press, 1958), I, 251–52. Hereinafter JLFA.

2. Jesse Lee, *A Short History of the Methodists* (Baltimore, 1810; facsimile ed., Rutland, Vt.: Academy Books, 1974), 130–31; also 130 for citation following.

3. The love feast will be a frequent topic in these pages. A simple meal of bread and water, it was a regular and familiar feature of early Methodist life. Like so much else in the Wesleyan lexicon, the love feast had been borrowed, in this case from the Moravians who had played a pivotal role in John and Charles Wesley's spiritual development. A ritual evocative of the common meals of the ancient church but not in common usage and hence not governed by ecclesiastical law

and practice or reserved to the clergy, the love feast suited the Wesleyan movement. It could be administered by Wesley's lay preachers and lay leaders. It also seemed to serve quasi-eucharistic functions and to carry some of the rich symbolic texture of communion. Part of the power in its symbolism derived from the practice common in the Methodist use of the rite, namely the sharing of testimony. This rather simple gesture—allowing each person, Black and white, male and female, rich and poor, old and young, to voice his/her spiritual journey—dramatized important Methodist affirmations: the essential equality of persons before God, the availability of pardoning grace, the acceptance and even love that brothers and sisters in the faith must accord one another irrespective of status, the responsibility they then had for one another, the part each was to play in Methodist community, and the unity then to be enjoyed in this new society. On the love feast, see Frank Baker, *Methodism and the Love Feast* (London: Epworth Press, 1967).

4. JLFA, I, 295 (Feb. 2, 1779); I, 245 (Aug. 4, 1777).

5. Frederick A. Norwood, *Sourcebook of American Methodism* (Nashville: Abingdon Press, 1982), 47. Dated Nov. 8, 1774.

6. "The Journals of Freeborn Garrettson," ed. Robert D. Simpson, transcript copy prepared for Academy Books, Aug. 5, 1781.

7. Emory S. Bucke, ed., *The History of American Methodism*, 3 vols. (New York and Nashville: Abingdon Press, 1964), I, 313.

8. The limitations on attendance at love feast and weekend situating of quarterly meetings were legislated in 1773 and 1780 respectively. See *Minutes of the Methodist Conferences Annually Held in America from 1773 to 1813 Inclusive* (New York, 1813), 6, 26. The perspective here set forth is largely drawn from Rhys Isaac, *The Transformation of Virginia, 1740–1790* (Chapel Hill: University of North Carolina Press, 1982); Donald G. Mathews, *Religion in the Old South* (Chicago: University of Chicago Press, 1977); and William H. Williams, *The Garden of Methodism* (Wilmington, Del.: Scholarly Resources, 1984).

9. "Journals," ed. Simpson.

10. "Journals," III for April 1, 20, 26, May 25, 27, 1790, in James Meacham Papers, 1788–1797. Manuscript Department, Duke University Library, Durham, N.C. Used with permission.

11. It should be noted at this point that Methodists did not enjoy sole possession either of fraternity's egalitarian or of its restrictive meaning. Other evangelical movements shared the egalitarian emphasis. Also fraternity had long been used for groups of clergy. Granting that, we still argue that the term is especially useful in highlighting certain dimensions of Methodist experience. In particular, we would note that the boundaries the term drew between clergy and laity were especially important for a Methodist ministry which at times seemed to have little more than the boundary itself to distinguish itself from the laity. Methodists took great pains to mark off the line between those "called" to preach from those called to exhort, to teach, to relate their experiences. The lines were fine but incredibly important.

12. "The Journal of Bishop Richard Whatcoat" in William Warren Sweet, *Religion on the American Frontier, 1783–1840*, 4 vols. (New York: Cooper Square Publishers, 1964; first published by University of Chicago Press, 1946, IV, *The Methodists*, 74, 75, 81, 82.

13. "The Edward Dromgoole Letters" in ibid., 132.

14. Ibid., 133–34.

15. Ibid., 136.

16. "Journals," VI for May 26, 1792, and IV for July 18, 1790, in James Meacham Papers, Duke.

17. Stith Mead, *A Short Account of the Experience and Labor of the Rev. Stith*

Mead (Lynchburg, 1829), 40, 41, 43, 47. Volume is owned by and used with permission of the General Commission on Archives and History, the United Methodist Church.

18. Ibid., 45.

19. "Journals," VI for Aug. 7, 1790, in James Meacham Papers, Duke.

20. "Journals," II for Feb. 10, 1789, and Various entries in III in James Meacham Papers, Duke. Appropriately, he also applied the phrase to a family gathering.

21. See, for example, Ezabiel Cooper's accounts liberally sampled in George A. Phoebus, *Beams of Light on Early Methodism in America* (New York: Phillips and Hunt, 1887).

22. James Meacham, "Journals," VI for Nov. 6, 1792, in James Meacham Papers, Duke.

23. JLFA, I, 402 (April 24, 1781).

24. Quoted by Jno. J. Tigert in *A Constitutional History of American Episcopal Methodism* (3d ed., Nashville: Publishing House of the Methodist Episcopal Church, South, 1908), 75.

25. JLFA, I, 116 (May 25, 1774).

26. JLFA, II, 469–70 (May 25, 1805).

27. JLFA, III, 112–13.

28. The jumble is readily observed at its source, the first *Discipline*. By comparing the *Discipline* with the Wesleyan source from which it was drawn, "The Large Minutes," we can see the Christmas Conference struggling over how to adjust the Wesleyan schema and terms to the churchly functions now envisioned (see Tigert, *Constitutional History*, Appendix VII). An interesting study is the Conference's disposition of the language concerning the helper, the workhorse and effective minister in Wesley's scheme of lay workers. In the first *Discipline*, the Conference apparently did not know what to do with the helper, did not know how the helper fit into the episcopal array of ministries, did not know whether to equate helper with deacon or elder (Questions 32–34). And so a section on "a helper" followed the list of duties of superintendent (the original term for bishop), elder, and deacon. There and throughout the *Discipline*, the Conference left with the helper all the ministerial prerogatives, duties, and rules that gave shape to ministry in the Wesleyan scheme. In short, Conference did not know how to manage the Wesleyan language. To elders and deacons had been given—by very brief entries—the newly acquired ritual functions. To helpers had been left the guts of Methodism. In the 1787 *Discipline*, the helper's duties and responsibilities became "the Directions given to a Preacher." This partially rectified the 1784 confusion, but only partially. The Wesleyan and episcopal language and understandings were really more juxtaposed than integrated.

The point, here, is not that conference did not know what ministry was. The struggles with Strawbridge and certainly from Fluvanna on suggest that Methodists knew precisely what they must do and felt its urgency keenly. The point is that they had one language with which to talk about ministry and adopted a second. To both of these they felt deep obligations. That understates it: they were prisoners to these languages. Neither set, without substantial lexical reworking, sufficed.

29. JLFA, I, 476 (Dec. 18, 1784).

30. See E. Dale Dunlap, "The United Methodist System of Itinerant Ministry," *Occasional Papers* 30 (Jan. 15, 1980).

31. See Donald M. Scott, *From Office to Profession: The New England Ministry, 1750–1850* (Philadelphia: University of Pennsylvania Press, 1978). Professionalization occurred later for Methodists than Scott suggests it did for Congregationalists.

2. From Quarterly to Camp Meeting

1. George A. Phoebus, *Beams of Light on Early Methodism in America* (New York: Phillips and Hunt, 1887), 204.

2. Thomas Coke, *Extracts of the Journals of . . . Thomas Coke* (Dublin, 1816), April 2, 1791, 174. Compare this response to the North Carolina conference with those for Georgia of March 16, 171, and of Virginia, April 20, 175; see also similar remarks on conferences for 1796, 232, 235.

3. On the dating of the camp meeting see Charles A. Johnson, *The Frontier Camp Meeting, Religion's Harvest Time* (Dallas: Southern Methodist University Press, 1955), 25–32. After reviewing various claimants, Johnson remarks, "Part of the difficulty is, of course, one of definition" (30). He concludes: "Yet the dispute about dates is relatively unimportant; many camp meetings may have taken place in the back country prior to the Second Great Awakening. The significant point is that they did not achieve universal popularity or standard form until after 1799" (31–32). We would concur but add that one set of precedents (which Johnson treats fully) does explain why the camp meeting became the Methodist religious expression.

4. For perceptive commentary on the difficulties in Methodism's transition from an "eschatologically oriented mission" to one "subtly bent into a civilizing mission," see Lester B. Scherer, *Ezekiel Cooper, 1763–1847* (Lake Junaluska: Commission on Archives and History, 1968), 190ff. American Methodism inherited from Wesley and British Methodism a preoccupation with the old ways. The power of these trans-Atlantic frequencies may well have minimized the capacity of the American leadership to monitor and respond to domestic signals. I am indebted to Donald G. Mathews for the notion of the camp meeting as metaphor. See his essay "Evangelical America"—The Methodist Ideology," in *Rethinking Methodist History* (Nashville: Kingswood Books/United Methodist Publishing House, 1985), 91–99.

5. William Warren Sweet, *Religion in the Development of American Culture, 1765–1840* (New York: Charles Scribner's Sons, 1952). The camp meeting is analyzed within a section on revivalism of a chapter devoted to "Barbarism vs. Revivalism." What makes these pages, 148–153, of more than just passing significance is a set of hypotheses to which this book is devoted: religion has laid the foundations of American culture; that office was performed by the religious conquest of the successive American frontiers; in this survival of the moralizers, adaptation to frontier conditions was key to the culture-forming capacity and hence growth of religious groups; the Protestantism that reached the masses was not the eastern, elitist, Presbyterian-Congregational variety but the Baptist-Methodist-Disciple-Cumberland-Presbyterian type; this second, American culture-forming, typical, expression of Protestantism Sweet illustrates and epitomizes with the camp meeting. See also Sweet's assessment in William Warren Sweet, *Religion on the American Frontier, 1783–1840* 4 vols. (New York: Cooper Square Publishers, 1964; first published by University of Chicago Press, 1946), IV. *The Methodists,* 68–69; *The Story of Religion in America,* rev. ed. (New York: Harper & Brothers, Publishers, 1939), 327–335; and *Revivalism in America* (New York: Charles Scribner's Sons, 1944), 129–33; in all of which the camp meeting is treated as frontier phenomenon. In William Warren Sweet, *Methodism in American History* (rev. ed., New York: Abingdon Press, 1954), on the other hand, the camp meeting is given scant attention and viewed as a national Methodist institution, 159–60, 333.

6. As illustrative of this impression see Winthrop S. Hudson, *Religion in*

America, 3d ed. (New York: Charles Scribner's Sons, 1981), 136–40; William G. McLoughlin, *Revivals, Awakenings, and Reform* (Chicago: University of Chicago Press, 1978), 131ff. Camp meetings are treated as national Methodist affairs by Robert T. Handy in *A History of the Churches in the United States and Canada* (Oxford: Oxford University Press, 1976), 167, and Sydney E. Ahlstrom in *A Religious History of the American People* (New Haven: Yale University Press, 1972), 437. Theodore L. Agnew, *The History of American Methodism,* 3 vols. (New York and Nashville: Abingdon Press, 1964), I, 507–23, treats camp meetings under the general rubric of "Methodism on the Frontier." However, Agnew does not so delimit the phenomenon. So also Frederick A. Norwood in *The Story of American Methodism* (Nashville: Abingdon Press, 1974), permits certain regional coloration to the camp meeting but does not confine it to the frontier.

　7. Johnson, *Frontier Camp Meeting,* vii, 7, 211, 98, 242.

　8. Ibid., 83–84, 86–87, 38, 51.

　9. Ibid., vii.

　10. Ibid., 100.

　11. John B. Boles, *The Great Revival, 1787–1805: The Origins of the Southern Evangelical Mind* (Lexington: University Press of Kentucky, 1972). Boles views the revival as a regional affair; dependent upon personnel, theology and techniques from the East; conditioned by society-wide crisis and anticipation; coincidentally sparked by the conversions and camp meetings of James McGready and a cohort of Presbyterians influenced by him; and setting loose a blaze that "swept back over the entire South with amazing rapidity, even seeping into the contiguous portions of the Ohio territory, western Pennsylvania and Maryland. By almost instantaneously overrunning the South, the Great Revival proved itself to be more than a mere frontier aberration" (70). He traces the appropriation of the camp meeting by the Methodists but is primarily concerned with southern religion as a whole and "why and how the revival developed" (52n).

　12. Dickson D. Bruce, *And They Sang Hallelujah: Plain-Folk Camp Meeting Religion, 1800-1845* (Knoxville: University of Tennessee Press, 1974). Bruce features the camp meeting as folk ritual, central in the phenomenology of Southern religious experience, an important part of frontier society. He is concerned with its choreography.

　13. Donald G. Mathews, *Religion in the Old South* (Chicago: University of Chicago Press, 1977). See also Robert T. Handy, *A Christian America,* 2d ed. (New York: Oxford University Press, 1984), Martin E. Marty, *Righteous Empire* (New York: The Dial Press, 1970), and McLoughlin, *Revivals, Awakenings, and Reform,* for treatment of evangelicalism's efforts at empire.

　14. *The Journal and Letters of Francis Asbury,* 3 vols., ed. Elmer T. Clark et al. (Nashville: Abingdon Press, 1958), III, 255. Letter to George Roberts, of Baltimore, dated Dec. 30, 1802. Hereinafter JLFA.

　15. JLFA, III, 251. Letter to Thornton Fleming, dated Dec. 2, 1802. Utilitarianism or pragmatism is clearly at play. Asbury said, "I wish you would also hold campmeetings; they have never been tried without success. To collect such a number of God's people together to pray, and the ministers to preach, and the longer they stay, generally, the better—this is field fighting, this is fishing with a large net" (ibid). Compare this June 3, 1803, account to Charles Atmore: "The present year is marked with great grace to the inhabitants of the United States. Great things have been done in the western states of Tennessee, Kentucky, and Ohio, by meetings held by encampments for several days and nights together. These meetings have obtained in Georgia, South and North Carolina, Virginia, Maryland, and Delaware" (JLFA, III, 261).

　16. Johnson points out that the adoption was never formalized, "that the camp

meeting was never an official institution of that denomination but only an "extra occasion in the economy of Methodism" (*Frontier Camp Meeting,* 6). It was, he says, "never an 'official' practice of the Methodist Episcopal Church. No church body ever adopted it; no laws were ever passed concerning it. There is no mention of this revival weapon in the Journal indexes of the general conferences, and but few references to it are to be found in the annual conference reports between 1800 and 1845. Nor do the many editions of the *Methodist Discipline* contain any rules to govern the camp meetings. Circuit riders never answered any formal questions concerning it in the quarterly conference" (ibid., 81).

17. On dilemmas of institutionalization see Thomas F. O'Dea, *The Sociology of Religion* (Englewood Cliffs, N.J.: Prentice-Hall, Inc., 1966), 90–97.

18. Jesse Lee, *A Short History of the Methodists* (Baltimore, 1810; facsimile ed., Rutland, Vt.: Academy Books, 1974), 59. Cf. accounts by Devereux Jarratt, Thomas Saunders, John Dickens, and Thomas Rankin reproduced in JLFA, I, 207–24.

19. *Minutes of the Methodist Conference Annually Held in America from 1773 to 1813 Inclusive* (New York, 1813), 26.

20. See preceding quotation from Lee and virtually any Methodist journal of the period. Lee observed, "Before this plan was adopted the quarterly meetings were generally held on the week days" (*Short History,* 71). The British pattern seems to have been more varied. The quarterly meetings and love feasts noted by Wesley are typically one-day affairs. See *The Journal of the Rev. John Wesley,* 9 vols., ed. Nehemiah Curnock (London: Epworth Press, 1909–1916), III, 491 (Aug. 22, 1750); VI, 31 (July 12, 1774), 282 (June 6, 1780); and VII, 181 (July 3, 1786), 290 (June 1787).

21. The journals of itinerants document the pattern. Among the best descriptions are those given by Ezekiel Cooper, some of which are reproduced by Phoebus in *Beams of Light.* Something of the pattern and the power of the second day is indicated in this statement: "Love-feast began between nine and ten o'clock, and held till after eleven o'clock; then the sacrament of the Lord's Supper was administered; public preaching began after twelve o'clock. We had a glorious time, especially in the close of our meeting. The power of God came down in the most powerful manner that I have ever seen in the state of New Jersey. It is said to have been the greatest time that has ever been known in this circuit. All ranks appeared to be in tears; many were overcome in such a manner that they could scarcely stand; some found Jesus, one man crying out to the congregation to help him to praise the Lord, for he had found him whom his soul loved. this increased the flame, and it ran through the house as fire among stubble. Soon as he ceased to speak a boy of about sixteen years of age broke out in prayer, after which we concluded our meeting" (78–79). See also for the year 1785, 27, 36, 38; for 1786, 61–63; for 1787, 78–90. For a decade later see the "Journal of Benjamin Lakin" in Sweet, *The Methodists,* 215, 216, 217, 220, 223, 224–25, 225. *The Experience and Travels of Mr. Freeborn Garrettson* (Philadelphia: Parry Hall, 1791) and the newly issued fuller version entitled *American Methodist Pioneer, The Life and Journals of The Rev. Freeborn Garrettson, 1752–1827* ed. Robert Drew Simpson (Rutland, Vt.: Academy Books, 1984) attest this pattern. See, for instance, entries for April 18–19, Aug. 7–8, Aug. 12–13, Aug. 19–20, and Nov. 11–12, 1780; April 16–17, Aug. 5–6, Oct. 30–31, and Nov. 4–3, 1781; and Jan. 5–6, Jan. 12–13, Jan. 19–20, Feb. 2–3, Oct. 21–22, Oct. 26–27, and Nov. 2–3, 1782. In 1783 and after Garrettson routinely refers to "both days."

22. See, in the Simpson edition, the entry for April 18–19, 1780. Asbury, who attended, converted Garrettson's claim into statistics. "Our little chapel with galleries, held about seven hundred; but there were I judge near one thousand peo-

ple" (JLFA, I, 345). The Anglican clergymen Samuel Magaw and Hugh Neill also participated. See Aug. 12–13, Aug. 19–20, Nov. 11–12 for estimates.

23. On the world the gentry made, see Rhys Isaac, *The Transformation of Virginia, 1740–1790* (Chapel Hill: University of North Carolina Press, 1982); Mathews, *Religion in the Old South.*

24. *Journals of Freeborn Garrettson*, Simpson ed., Aug. 5, 6, 1781. Garrettson continued, "The evening was spent in preaching and exhorting."

25. Phoebus, *Beams of Light*, 142. It is important to accent the "spiritual" quality of the egalitarian message of Methodism. Forms of segregation appeared early. For instance, in another quarterly meeting that same year which drew a large crowd, the Blacks were sent to the barns (137), Still the outdoor meetings, spatially open, compromised the inclusive and universal message of Methodism less than the confined quarters of a meeting house which for a variety of reasons fostered not only segregation, which came very early, but the drawing of all sorts of lines. As private space a building invited division into us and them; field or forest as public space permitted "trespass."

26. On the love feast see note 3 in chapter 1 and *History of American Methodism*, I, 307–17.

27. In early *Disciplines* these are not gathered. For instance, in the 1798 *Discipline* administrative functions are partially outlined in Chap. I, X "Of the Duties of those who have the Charge of Circuits"; licensing tasks are addressed in XXI "Of the Local Preachers"; financial obligations under Chap. II, V, "Of the Qualification and Duty of the Stewards of Circuits," *The Doctrines and Discipline of the Methodist Episcopal Church in America. With Explanatory Notes by Thomas Coke and Francis Asbury* (Philadelphia, 1798); facsimile edition entitled *The Methodist Discipline of 1798*, ed. Frederick A. Norwood (Rutland, Vt.: Academy Books, 1979). For the historic and continuing powers of the quarterly meeting see Nolan B. Harmon, *The Organization of the Methodist Church*, 2d ed. (Nashville: The Methodist Publishing House, 1962), "The Quarterly Conference," 148ff.

28. JLFA, I, 413 (Nov. 3, 1781).

29. Phoebus, *Beams of Light*, 27.

30. JLFA, I, 525 (Nov. 1786). Unfortunately, the journals tend to record only the names of the principals at these occasions. Where travel and weather conditions permitted, a quarterly meeting for which Asbury was expected would have tended to draw heavily. Others were doubtless much smaller. But it was not unusual for there to be a handful of preachers plus other leaders. Ezekial Cooper was somewhat more careful to record names than others. See, for instance, Phoebus, *Beams of Light*, 62, for this account of a quarterly meeting Feb. 11–12, 1787, at which Whatcoat, Abbott, Sparks, and Cooper preached and Brush also participated.

31. "The Journal of Bishop Richard Whatcoat," in Sweet, *The Methodists*, 73–122, because it is so spare, illustrates nicely the "collective" character of Methodist ministry.

32. *Experience and Travels of Mr. Freeborn Garrettson*, 67.

33. James Meacham Journals, II, Feb. 10, 1789, Feb. 19, 1789; III, Feb. 19, 1790, Mar. 5, 1790, Mar. 11, 1790; Mar. 26, 1790, Ap. 8, 1790, May 8, 1790; and IV, July 18, 1790. in James Meacham Papers, 1788–1797. Manuscript Department, Duke University Library, Durham, N.C. Used with permission.

34. JLFA, I, 295 (Feb. 2, 1779). Compare an entry for Aug. 4, 1777 (I, 245), for the Frederick quarterly meeting: "The next day our meeting began with a love feast; and we had a powerful melting time." Or of a Maryland quarterly meeting Nov. 3–4, 177 (I, 251) at which there "were many friends from Virginia, and the congregation was very large." "It was a powerful, melting time, and concluded in

the spirit of love." The estimation was an exceedingly common one and was, of course, used for other occasions than the quarterly meeting.

35. Journals for July 11, 12, 1789 and Aug. 1, 2, 1789. Compare the quarterly meeting-revivals of 1787 described by Lee, *Short History*, 130–34.

36. *Lectures on Revivals of Religion*, ed. William G. McLoughlin (Cambridge, Mass.: Harvard University Press, 1960). Chapter II bears the aforementioned title; the remainder of the volume details what fosters or inhibits revival.

37. Thomas Morrell, *Journal, 1789–1809*. Copy of mss journal. Drew University, Archives and History Center. Entry for May 1800. Lee noted, "While the general conference was sitting in Baltimore, the preachers were very useful in the beginning of a glorious revival in that place." *Short History*, 271. Cf. JLFA, II, 231, and *Those Incredible Methodists: A History of the Baltimore Conference*, ed. Gordon Pratt Baker (Baltimore: Commission on Archives and History, the Baltimore Conference, 1972), 89–90, for spread.

38. Lee, *Short History*, 138–40. JLFA, I, 537 (April 18, 1787) and I, 625 (Feb. 15, 1790). For many more he speaks of the public preaching without speculating about the long-term effects thereof.

39. JLFA, I, 594–96, 598.

40. These begin with volume 25 (1802) and abate in volume 28 (1805). Included are letters from Methodists (Asbury, Cooper, Stith Mead, Thomas Ware, Daniel Hall, Richard Sneath, William Colbert, Hamilton Jefferson, John Hagerty, Seely Bunn, and James Jenkins) to Coke, letters between other Methodist acquaintances, and reprints of accounts from non-Methodists.

41. *Extracts of Letters . . .* (New York: Published by Ezekiel Cooper and John Wilson for the Methodist Connection in the United States, 1805). Many are from presiding elders and constitute the religious state of the district so frequently demanded by Asbury. Except for the Kentucky meetings the quarterly and camp meetings are in territory that Methodism worked. It would be difficult to read this volume attentively and argue that the camp meeting was a frontier affair.

42. For characterization of Lee's history and discussion of Lee's publication after being denied a Methodist imprimatur, see Kenneth E. Rowe, "Counting the Converts: Progress Reports as Church History," in *Rethinking Methodist History*, 11–17.

43. The first of these in 1776 is cited above. A subsequent revival in the same area occurred in 1787. Read in its entirety, *Short History*, 129–33, it is a striking attestation of the quarterly meeting as revival. Just to illustrate: "The most remarkable work of all was in Sussex, and Brunswick circuits, where the meetings would frequently continue for five or six hours together, and some times all night.

"At one quarterly meeting held at Mabry's chapel in Brunswick circuit, on the 25th and 26th of July, the power of God was among the people in an extraordinary manner: some hundreds were awakened; and it was supposed that above one hundred souls were converted at the meeting which continued for two days, i.e., on Thursday and Friday. Some thousands of people attended meeting at that place on that occasion.

"The next quarterly-meeting was held at *Jones's* chapel in *Sussex* county. . . . " The revival narrative continues. For the 1789 quarterly meeting revival see 145–55. Annual conference in 1788 and the General Conference in 1800 are the narrative center of the other two accounts (138–40, 271–75). Others mentioned, not described and for which a quarterly meeting role is neither affirmed nor denied, are Jarratt's 1770–71 (43–44), a 1774 Maryland eastern shore (49), one in 1781 affecting the Peninsula, Va. and N.C. (77), a 1784 frontier revival (89), and those associated with Lee's own labors in N.E. (216ff.)

44. *The Methodist Magazine*, 25, 217.

45. Ibid., 25, 262–63. J. Chappell to Edwards dated Oct. 23, 1801.

46. For revival report from an annual meeting see below. On the revival role of quarterly meeting see *The Methodist Magazine,* 25, 521–23, Stith Mead to Coke; Vol. 26, 370ff. for reports by Thomas Ware and Daniel Hall to Coke on Delaware and Albemarle respectively, Richard Sneath's to Coke and Hamilton Jefferson to Coke. Camp meeting reports abound, including one reported in a subsequent letter of Stith Mead, vol. 26, 419.

47. Quarterly meetings, pp. 17–18; annual meetings, 24–26, 28–30; encampment, 37–39; nine-day quarterly meeting, 49–50; six-day quarterly meeting, 101–102; quarterly meetings as camp meetings, pp. 54–55, 108–109. A single report that juxtaposes quarterly meetings and camp meetings is William P. Chandler's of Aug. 1805. Compare JLFA, III, 327–31.

48. *The Methodist Magazine,* 25, 422–223.

49. *Sketches of The Life and Travels of Rev. Thomas Ware . . . Written by Himself* (New York, 1842; facsimile edition published by the Holston Conference Task Force on the Celebration of the Bicentennial of American Methodism, 1984), 234. For Ware's retrospective linking of the quarterly meeting and revival see pp. 61, 62–69, 115, 164–67, 169, 175, 198, 217, 227–30, 231, 233–34.

3. Views of the Nation

1. *The Journal and Letters of Francis Asbury,* 3 vols., ed. Elmer T. Clark et al. (Nashville: Abingdon Press, 1958), III, 566, Aug. 2, 1806. Hereinafter JLFA. The reader should note that the glass here permits the user to peer into Asbury's heart. In the prior chapter, the metaphor of glass as mirror was employed to understand the relation of the quarterly meeting to its reflection in camp meeting. Here, glass functions differently, as in Asbury's statement, as a device that permits the attentive observer to see through the appearances, through the body of Methodism, to its heart.

2. This contrast recurs through the journals of the early itinerants. This particular formulation is taken from *The Experience and Travels of Mr. Freeborn Garrettson* (Philadelphia: Parry Hall, 1791), 59.

3. JLFA, III, 480, Aug. 5, 1813.

4. In *People of Paradox* (New York: Vintage Books, 1973), Michael Kammen suggests that such ambiguities or contradictions more aptly capture the dynamics of American experience than the more typically drawn contrasts between Old World and New and the presumption of linear progression from the one to the other. The contrasts lurked within.

5. R. Laurence Moore, *Religious Outsiders and the Making of Americans* (New York: Oxford University Press, 1986). In Moore's estimation, the stance as religious outsider becomes the vehicle for claiming status as American and ultimately for the constituting of American society itself. American religious movements come into being then with the sort of ambivalence investigated here.

6. See Andrew M. Greeley, *The Denominational Society* (Glenview, Ill.: Scott, Foresman & Company, 1972), 76 and William H. Swatos, Jr., "Beyond Denominationalism: Community and Culture in American Religion," *Journal for the Scientific Study of Religion,* 20 (Sept. 1981), 219. For sustained criticism of H. Richard Niebuhr's notion that religious movements inevitably develop from sect to denomination, see Alan W. Eister, "H. Richard Niebuhr and the Paradox of Religious Organization: A Radical Critique," *Beyond the Classics?,* ed. Charles Y. Glock and

Phillip E. Hammond (New York: Harper & Row, Publishers, 1973), 355–408, and James A. Beckford, *Religious Organization: A Trend Report and Bibliography* published initially as *Current Sociology/La Sociologie Contemporaine* 21 (1973/ 2), 15.

7. Fred J. Hood, *Reformed America: The Middle and Southern States, 1783–1837* (University: University of Alabama Press, 1980), 34. See also Sacvan Bercovitch, *The American Jeremiad* (Madison: University of Wisconsin Press, 1978); John F. Berens, *Providence & Patriotism in Early America, 1640–1815* (Charlottesville: University Press of Virginia, 1978); Nathan O. Hatch, *The Sacred Cause of Liberty* (New Haven: Yale University Press, 1977), and the considerable literature on civil religion.

8. See Paul C. Nagel, *One Nation Indivisible: The Union in American Thought, 1776–1861* (New York: Oxford University Press, 1964); Paul C. Nagel, *This Sacred Trust: American Nationality, 1798–1898* (New York: Oxford University Press, 1971); Cushing Strout, *The New Heavens and New Earth: Political Religion in America* (New York: Harper & Row, Publishers, 1974); Catherine L. Albanese, *Sons of the Fathers: The Civil Religion of the American Revolution* (Philadelphia: Temple University Press, 1976).

9. Robert Paine, *Life and Times of William McKendree*, 2 vols. (Nashville: Publishing House of the Methodist Episcopal Church, South, 1874), I, 347–48.

10. Wade C. Barclay and J. Tremayne Copplestone, *History of Methodist Missions*, 4 vols. (New York: Board of Missions, the Methodist Church, 1949–1973), II, 8. Frederick A. Norwood, *The Story of American Methodism* (Nashville: Abingdon Press, 1974), 186. C. C. Goen, "The 'Methodist Age' in American Church History," *Religion in Life,* 34 (Autumn, 1965), 566. Sidney E. Mead, *The Lively Experiment* (New York: Harper & Row, Publishers, 1963), 118.

11. The succession of changes in the *Discipline* is as follows. The second edition followed that of 1784 (published in 1785). The 1787 added the statement just cited. 1788 added "as also the extremities of the Western Settlements." 1789 made no change. 1790 adopted the change just mentioned. In addition references to the number of years since Methodist work began were appropriately altered. Then in 1798 Western Settlements became "western and eastern states." Disciplines were consulted in The Methodist Center, Drew University.

12. The comparison is most readily seen in the parallel arrangement of Discipline and Large Minutes in Jno. J. Tigert, *A Constitutional History of American Episcopal Methodism,* 3d ed. (Nashville: Publishing House of the Methodist Episcopal Church, South, 1908), 535.

13. Frank Baker observes of this alteration: "The American answer naturally disavowed any connection with the Church of England, and modified the closing phrase so as to describe more adequately the enormous mission field which confronted them. . . . " Frank Baker, "The Americanization of Methodism," *A.M.E. Zion Quarterly Review/Methodist History/News Bulletin* (April 1975), 18; this is *Methodist History* 13.

14. JLFA, III, 157–58, Feb. 8, 1797. Compare similar statements which are continental in their orientation if not always their terminology in II, 29, Oct. 2, 1794; 155, Mar. 4, 1798; III, 148–49, Nov. 1, 1796; 162, Aug. 29, 1797; 430, June 2, 1810; 456, Nov. 27, 1811; 476, 480, 482 in the Valedictory Address of Aug. 5, 1813; 563, Jan. 11, 1806; 568, Aug. 11, 1806. The pattern doubtless continues Asbury's orientation to America before it was nation, captured in entries like that for Jan. 27, 1779 in I, 294.

15. JLFA, II, 332, Apr. 5, 1802; 337, May 1, 1802; 342, June 5, 1802.

16. One target of such persecution was Freeborn Garrettson. His *The Experience and Travels of Mr. Freeborn Garrettson* recounts those adversities and indi-

cates how even well-placed and highly loyal American loyalists suffered under the Methodist banner.

17. Theodore C. Linn, "Religion and Nationalism: American Methodism and The New Nation in the Early National Period, 1766–1844," (Ph.D. diss., Drew University, 1971, 267, 76.

18. JLFA, III, 70–1, May 29, 1789. To be fair to Linn, I should note that he discerns three stages in Methodist providential interpretation of the nation: providential reading of the Revolution, the appropriation of the New England sacred history, and a full-fledged covenantal view (ibid., 90–91). The three views are only prefigured here.

19. See *Inaugural Addresses of the Presidents of the United States* (82d Congress, 2d Session, House Document No. 540), 1–2.

20. Gordon Pratt Baker, ed., *Those Incredible Methodists: A History of the Baltimore Conference* (Baltimore: Commission on Archives and History, the Baltimore Conference, 1972), 404.

21. For the availability of these views see Berens, *Providence and Patriotism,* and Robert T. Handy, *A Christian America,* 2d ed. (New York: Oxford University Press, 1984).

22. *Minutes of the Methodist Conferences, 1773 to 1813* (New York, 1813), 163.

23. Ibid., 164.

24. John Dow, *A Discourse Delivered by Request July 4, 1806 in the Methodist Church at Belleville* (Newark, 1806), 16–21.

25. Ibid., 21–22.

26. Thomas Coke and Francis Asbury, *The Doctrines and Discipline of the Methodist Episcopal Church in America with Explanatory Notes* (Philadelphia, 1798), 140.

27. Ibid., 37, 38, 45, 53.

28. "The Address of the General Conference to the Members of the Methodist Episcopal Church in the United States of America," in Nathan Bangs, *A History of the Methodist Episcopal Church,* 4 vols. (New York, 1860), II, 325–26. Compare the 1805 Virginia Addresses to Methodist People, JLFA, III, 310, 314, Mar. 8, 1805, and May 7, 1805.

29. Coke and Asbury, *Doctrines and Discipline,* 159, 167.

30. JLFA, I, 606, July 31, 1789.

31. JLFA, III, 109, Jan. 1, 1792. The term seems to be something of an evangelical commonplace, a useful way of connecting one's own religious efforts and body with the larger reality of the church. It certainly was not unique to Methodists nor to North Americans. It recurs through the hymnody of evangelical Protestantism. This discussion does not assume Zion to be a Methodist distinctive. We are only concerned with how Methodists used the term. Incidentally, it may have functioned for early Methodists as a useful euphemism, allowing them to leave "church" to the Anglicans but to claim through its biblical antecedent all the essentials of church. Pilmore, for instance, uses the term "Zion" frequently for the spiritual reality brought into being by the Methodists and reserves the word "church" for Anglicanism and Anglican buildings. For his references to 'Zion' see *The Journal of Joseph Pilmore,* ed. Frederick E. Maser and Howard T. Maag (Philadelphia: Historical Society of the Philadelphia Annual Conference, 1969), 32, 37, 38, 67, 73, 74, 91, 101, 102, 108, 109, 110, 111, 127, 158, 179, 189.

32. *The Arminian Magazine,* II, 202, "An Extract of a Letter from James Haw, Elder . . . to Bishop Asbury."

33. George A. Phoebus, *Beams of Light on Early Methodism in America* (New York: Phillips and Hunt, 1887), 9.

34. Bangs, III, 73, 90.

35. Bangs, III, 262.
36. Bangs, II, 39.
37. Bangs, III, 64.
38. JLFA, III, 287. Freeborn Garrettson, *Substance of the Semi-Centennial Sermon before the New York Annual Conference* (New York, 1827).
39. JLFA, III, 372, Dec. 28, 1802.
40. For some attempts in these directions see Frank Baker, "The Americanization of Methodism"; Douglas R. Chandler, "Towards the Americanizing of Methodism," *Methodist History*, 13 (Oct. 1974), 3–16; Linn, "Religion and Nationalism"; Jaroslav Pelikan, "Methodism's Contribution to America," in Emory S. Bucke, ed., *The History of American Methodism*, 3 vols. (New York and Nashville: Abingdon Press, 1964), III, 596–614; Goen, "The 'Methodist Age' in American Church History"; Robert Handy, "Methodism's Contributions to American Life," *Christian Advocate*, 10/7 (April 7, 1966), 7–8; Donald G. Mathews, "The Second Great Awakening as an Organizing Process, 1780–1830," in *Religion in American History*, ed. John M. Mulder and John F. Wilson (Englewood Cliffs, N.J.: Prentice-Hall, Inc., 1978), 199–217; virtually any of the works of William Warren Sweet; and John Abernathy Smith, "How Methodism Became a National Church in the United States," *Methodist History*, 20 (Oct. 1981), 13–28.
41. JLFA, III, 566.
42. See especially Goen, "The 'Methodist Age' in American Church History" for discussion of this point and the literature which makes it.

4. The Southern Accent of American Methodism

1. *A Form of Discipline for the Ministers, Preachers and Members of the Methodist Episcopal Church in America* (New York: 1787), 3–4. Compare *The Book of Discipline of the United Methodist Church, 1988* (Nashville: United Methodist Publishing House, 1988), 9. For participants in the contest over priority, see the *Report of the Joint Commission Representing the Methodist Episcopal Church, The Methodist Episcopal Church, South, the Methodist Protestant Church, The Origin of Methodism in America* (Chicago: Press of the Methodist Book Concern, 1916). On the title page, the volume is *Origin of American Methodism: Report of . . .* H. K. Carroll's *The First Methodist Society in America* (New York: Published for the Methodist Historical Society of the City of New York, 1916), also summarizes the controversy. See also Edwin Schell, "Beginnings in Maryland and America," in *Those Incredible Methodists: A History of the Baltimore Conference*, ed. Gordon Pratt Baker (Baltimore: Commission on Archives and History, the Baltimore Conference, 1972), 16–17.
2. The hold that this contest has had over the Methodist historical imagination is well illustrated in the priority given the issue in George Bourne's "A Comprehensive History of American Methodism," a section subjoined to his *The Life of the Rev. John Wesley, A.M.* (Baltimore: George Dobbin & Murphy, 1807), 321–51. Bourne recounted the endeavors of Embury and Webb and then affirmed: "At this period Mr. Strawbridge, a local preacher from Ireland, settled in Frederick county, Maryland, and formed several societies. It has long been a question the curious who are anxious to know every circumstance which is connected with the commencement of Methodism in the United States; whether the first society was established, and whether the first house of worship was erected in Maryland or in New-York; whether the old log house in which Mr. Strawbridge preached on Pipe Creek, was not antecedent to the building which was used by captain Webb and

Mr. Embury? After the most accurate research, the information which I have procured induces me to believe, that a Methodist society was formed at New-York at least nine or twelve months previous to the first which was collected by Mr. Strawbridge; and there can be no doubt, that the room, and even the rigging house were devoted to the publick worship of God in New-York, prior to the use of the log house of Pipe Creek" (p. 322). He then reproduced letters to Wesley by T.T. of April 11, 1768, and by T.B. of May 1, 1769, supporting that claim.

For biographical details on Bourne (1780–1845) see H. Shelton Smith, *In His Image, But . . .* (Durham: Duke University Press, 1972), 61–66, and Theodore Bourne, "George Bourne, The Pioneer of American Antislavery," *Methodist Quarterly Review*, LXIV (Jan. 1882). Standard Methodist reference volumes do not include him. That may be because he became Presbyterian and later Dutch Reformed. He left the South because of slavery. The *Dictionary of American Biography*, 21 vols. (New York: Charles Scribner's Sons, 1928–37), II, does not refer to a Methodist phase of his career or include this particular work in his bibliography. The *National Union Catalog* does place this work within his corpus.

3. Jesse Lee, *A Short History of the Methodists* (Baltimore, 1810; facsimile ed., Rutland, Vt.: Academy Books, 1974), 24, 25.

4. George C. M. Roberts, "Introduction of Methodism into America," *Methodist Quarterly Review, South*, 13 (Jan. 1859), 44–54. After arguing the case for New York and Baltimore beginnings in 1760, Roberts proposed "that we celebrate the CENTENARY OF METHODISM some time during the winter of 1860," p. 54. Hilary T. Hudson, *The Methodist Armor* (1st ed., 1892; rev. and enl. ed., Nashville: Printed for the Author, Publishing House of the Methodist Episcopal Church, South, 1895), 12. Compare the concession of New York priority made in the "Knoxville District Centenary Address," *The Christian Advocate* (Nashville), 44 (March 1, 1884), p. 6.

5. Holland N. McTyeire, *A History of Methodism* (Nashville: Southern Methodist Publishing House, 1884, 1924), 271–72. For discussion of the case for Strawbridge and Maryland's shaping of American Methodism, see 253–57.

6. *Journal of the Twenty-Seventh Delegated General Conference of the Methodist Episcopal Church*, 1916, pp. 1503–1505. See the appendix for further description of the Joint Commission on the Origin of American Methodism and its work.

7. Schell, "Beginnings in Maryland and America," 5–14.

8. William Warren Sweet, *Methodism in American History*, (rev. ed., New York and Nashville: Abingdon Press, 1953), 65. Sweet went on to affirm, "This emphasis is doubtless due to the fact that it was here that Wesley's missionaries spent much of their time, while the work in the southern colonies was carried on largely by the irregulars, such as Strawbridge and Williams, or by the native American preachers."

9. Southern religious history has prospered over the last decade. See, for instance, Donald G. Mathews, *Religion in the Old South* (Chicago: University of Chicago Press, 1977), E. Brooks Holifield, *The Gentlemen Theologians* (Durham: Duke University Press, 1978), Anne C. Loveland, *Southern Evangelicals and the Social Order, 1800–1860* (Baton Rouge: Louisiana State University Press; 1980), Albert J. Raboteau, *Slave Religion* (Oxford, New York, Toronto, Melbourne: Oxford University Press, 1978), and several volumes associated with Sam Hill, including Samuel S. Hill, ed., *Encyclopedia of Religion in the South* (Macon, Ga.: Mercer University Press, 1984).

Perforce, historians continue the long debate about whether and how southern religion differs from American religion as a whole, and if different, in what ways. Note David E. Harrell's remarks in the "Introduction" to his edited volume, *Varie-*

ties of Southern Evangelicalism (Macon, Ga.: Mercer University Press, 1981): "With the exception of the distinctive black religious experience in the South, there is little that is qualitatively unique about southern Evangelicalism. . . . But if the southern religious experience is not qualitatively distinct, it is quantitatively. . . . Southern Evangelicals have been more individualistic, less confident in social reform, more literal in their views·of the Bible, more moved by personal religious experience; southern religion has been more given to sectarianism in the twentieth century—or so it is argued in this book. More obvious, the South has been the most solidly evangelical section of the country," 2. For further efforts to define southern religion, see Samuel S. Hill's essay in the same volume, "The Shape and Shapes of Popular Southern Piety," 89–114, and Donald Mathews's entry on "Evangelicalism" in Hill, *Encyclopedia of Religion*, 243–44.

10. Frederick A. Norwood provides a most discerning discussion of what he terms "the peculiar pattern of growth," the "irregular and sporadic" spread of Methodism. For him as for many northern Methodists, the southern character of early Methodism is a problem to be explained; Norwood, *The Story of American Methodism* (Nashville: Abingdon Press, 1974), 74–75. Norwood assigns these reasons: that the Revolution disrupted Methodist life unevenly, heavily in New York; that in the North, Methodism competed with an established Congregationalism and an entrenched Presbyterianism; that Methodism prospered within the Anglican network and particularly where Anglican leadership welcomed it; that various demographic factors affected Methodist advances.

Nor is Lawrence Sherwood concerned with how southern origins may have affected the movement as a whole. Instead, like so many historians before and after, he presents Methodism as a national movement; Sherwood, "Growth and Spread, 1785–1804," in Emory S. Bucke, ed., *History of American Methodism*, 3 vols. (New York and Nashville: Abingdon Press, 1964), I, 360–418. The governing sentiment is indicated in the following: "The growth of the Methodist Episcopal Church during its first twenty years of existence is phenomenal. From its rather limited beginning in 1785, the church expanded in geographical area and in membership until it became a major influence in both the religious and social aspects of the new nation," I, 361.

11. Henry Boehm, *Reminscences, Historical and Biographical* (New York, 1865), 57, quoted by William A. Williams, *The Garden of American Methodism: The Delmarva Peninsula, 1769–1820* (Wilmington, Del.: Scholarly Resources, 1984), xi–xiii.

12. Schell, "Beginnings in Maryland and America," 2.

13. Garber prefaced this remark in William Warren Sweet, *Virginia Methodism: A History* (Richmond, Va.: Whittet & Shepperson, 1955), v, ix, 44. Sweet concurred, affirming, "Colonial Virginia was the first important seed plot of American Methodism." The sponsoring Committee on the Preparation of the History of the Virginia Annual Conference found one metaphor inadequate: "Virginia was the cradle of American Methodism, the original fertile seedplot from which John Wesley's disciples in America eventually spread Methodism into every state and almost every county of this great American nation."

14. Including Delaware and Maryland in the South (and perhaps even the area of Pennsylvania immediately adjacent) will seem questionable to persons accustomed to thinking of the Old South in terms of those colonies/states that adhered to the Confederacy. Alternatively we might term this Methodism eastern or Middle Atlantic. Two reasons suggest the southern designation. First, as William Williams has shown, the demographic, social and cultural realities that Methodism encountered in Delmarva peninsula closely resemble those described by Rhys Isaac and others for Virginia. This whole region was a slave culture, a factor to which this

paper turns much attention. Second, in the period during which Methodism planted itself, the regional identities and regional boundaries that would split the Union were not completely formed. Hence our use has a certain anachronistic quality. However, we judge it important, despite its imprecision, to employ the designation. See Rhys Isaac, *The Transformation of Virginia, 1740–1790* (Chapel Hill: University of North Carolina Press, 1982), Williams, *Garden of American Methodism*, Mathews, *Religion in the Old South*.

15. For conferences and statistics, see *Minutes of the Methodist Conferences Annually Held in America from 1773 to 1813 Inclusive* (New York, 1813). Lee, *Short History of the Methodists*, provides much the same information as would virtually any Methodist history. See, for instance, Bucke, *History of American Methodism*.

16. Lester J. Cappon, ed., *Atlas of Early American History: The Revolutionary Era, 1760–1790* (Princeton: Princeton University Press, 1976), 71.

17. Lee, *Short History of the Methodists*, 255.

18. See annual entries in *Minutes of the Methodist Conferences Annually Held in America from 1773 to 1813 Inclusive*. This analysis utilizes *Crowned Victors: The Memoirs of Over Four Hundred Methodist Preachers, Including the First Two Hundred and Fifty Who Died on This Continent*. Compiled by J. W. Hedges (Baltimore: Methodist Episcopal Book Depository, 1878), which gathered the memoirs down to 1829 from the *Annual Minutes* (thereafter confining itself to those of the Baltimore Conference). Of the 245 memoirs for national Methodism, 33 did not include a reference to place of nativity. The numbers are striking: 45, Virginia; 33, Maryland; 23, North Carolina; 16, New York; 15, New Jersey; 12, England/Britain; 10, South Carolina; 10, Ireland; 9, Delaware; 9, Massachusetts; 7, Pennsylvania; 7, Connecticut; 4, New Hampshire; 3, Tennessee; 2, Maine; 2, Georgia; 1, Missouri, Kentucky, Wales, Scotland, Europe. Those not given a nativity can be assumed to distribute themselves along the proportions indicated above, but probably derived overwhelmingly from the South because they were, for the most part, admitted on trial in the eighteenth century.

19. *The Journal and Letters of Francis Asbury*, 3 vols., ed. Elmer T. Clark et al. (Nashville: Abingdon Press, 1958), II, 55–56, Sept. 23, 1807 (hereinafter JLFA).

20. JLFA, II, 615, Sept. 10, 1809.

21. JLFA, II, 694, Feb. 16, 1812.

22. JLFA, II, 554, Sept. 4, 1807; 573, July 3, 1808; 615, Sept. 10, 1809.

23. JLFA, II, 481, Sept. 21, 23, 1805.

24. JLFA, II, 684, Sept. 4, 1811.

25. Excerpts from the Dromgoole materials in the Southern Historical Collection, Chapel Hill, can be found in William Warren Sweet, *Religion on the American Frontier, 1783–1840*, IV, *The Methodists* (Chicago: University of Chicago Press, 1946), 123–201.

26. William Warren Sweet, ed., *The Rise of Methodism in the West: Being the Journal of the Western Conference, 1800–1811* (New York and Nashville: Methodist Book Concern; Nashville, Dallas, Richmond: Smith & Lamar, 1920), 92–95. The list of those admitted on trial:

"William Ellington, born in the State of Georgia"
"Samuel Parker, a native of New Jersey"
"Joshua Oglesby"
"William Thompson, a native of Maryland"
"Adbel Coleman, a native of New York"
"William Houstin, a native of Virginia"
"Richard Browning"

"Peter Cartwright, a native of Virginia"
"Joseph Williams, a native of Pennsylvania"
"Miles Harper, a native of Virginia"
"Edmond Wilcox, a native of Virginia"
"Joshua Barnes"
"James Axley"
"Joshua Riggin"
"Thomas Lasley, a native of Virginia"
"Caleb Wesley Cloud, born . . . in the state of Delaware"
"Benjamin Edge"
"Obed Noland, a native of Virginia"

Of those unidentified by the conference secretary, I can find a state of origin only for Barnes—Maryland (Axley is identified as from Iowa but this may be a mistake); for the others cards do exist in the ministerial cardfile in the Archives Center, Drew University, but these cards and the brief memorials to which they lead provide no further information on states of origin. For those lacking a state of origin, the secretary indicated instead the quarterly meeting of that Western Conference which recommended the candidate for trial.

27. See *Minutes*, 243–48, for the appointments. I derived home states from *The Encyclopedia of World Methodism*, ed. Nolan B. Harmon et al., 2 vols. (Nashville: United Methodist Publishing House, 1974); Mathew Simpson, *Cyclopaedia of Methodism* (repr. of 1876 ed., New York: Gordon Press, 1977); obituaries in later volumes of the *Minutes* and in *The Christian Advocate*; the card file on Methodist ministers in the Archives Center, Drew University; identifications in JLFA, particularly, II, 135, 265; and Abel Stevens, *Memorials of the Introduction of Methodism into the Eastern States* (Boston: C. H. Peirce, 1848).

28. Lee, *A Short History of the Methodists*. Sweet said of Lee: "After Francis Asbury, Jesse Lee stands out most prominently in the first fifty years of American Methodist history," *Virginia Methodism*, 157.

29. See the editor's superb historiographical essay in Leonard Sweet, ed., *The Evangelical Tradition in America* (Macon: Mercer University Press, 1984), 1–86.

30. Perhaps, we shall argue, the evangelical (and Methodist) hold in the South is far more natural than we are sometimes taught.

The chapter's burden is threefold: to identify features of religious culture that, first, have a clear southern ambience; that, second, at least initially, typify southern Methodism (even if shared with other forms of evangelicalism and other denominations); and that, third, appear subsequently as continuing patterns in the national Methodist ethos. Under review, then, are aspects of southern Methodism that are regionally characteristic, distinguishing, and defining of the movement nationally. Two caveats. First, as will be patent to any who have worked this turf, features that shade into one another are here presented in sharp relief. None of the individual points here presented cannot be applied, perhaps with some qualification, to northern Methodists in the early period, to evangelicals generally, to British Wesleyans. I think we would find, however, that as a constellation they do not epitomize other movements. Second, since the chapter examines distinctive aspects of southern Methodism, it cannot and shall not treat dimensions of southern Methodism which, though vital, were largely shared. So, much known to be essential to early Methodism is intentionally omitted.

31. Rhys Isaac, *The Transformation of Virginia, 1740–1790* (Chapel Hill: University of North Carolina Press, 1982). Mathews, *Religion in the Old South*. Bertram Wyatt-Brown, *Honor and Violence in the Old South* (New York: Oxford

University Press, 1986) and *Southern Honor: Ethics and Behavior in the Old South* (New York: Oxford University Press, 1982).

32. Stith Mead, *A Short Account of the Experience and Labors of the Rev. Stith Mead* (Lynchburg, 1829), 47–48.

33. Mathews, *Religion in the Old South*, 1, 35. The citation is taken from JLFA, I, 346, April 23, 1780.

34. Williams, *The Garden of American Methodism*, 90.

35. See, for instance, Frank Baker, "The Status of Methodist Preachers in America, 1769–1791," in Russell E. Richey and Kenneth E. Rowe, eds., *Rethinking Methodist History* (Nashville: United Methodist Publishing House, 1985).

36. See the third point in this discussion.

37. See Donald G. Mathews, *Slavery and Methodism: A Chapter in American Morality* (Princeton: Princeton University Press, 1965). Compromise is Mathews's central category, figuring in the titles of five chapters. His later, more nuanced treatment of the issue in *Religion in the Old South* informs this essay. Compare also James D. Essig, *The Bonds of Wickedness: American Evangelicals Against Slavery, 1770–1808* (Philadelphia: Temple University Press, 1982).

38. A. T. Bledsoe, "The M.E. Churches, North and South," A Review of *History of the Organization of the Methodist Episcopal Church, South* by A. H. Redford in *The Southern Review*, 10 (April 1872), 382–421, p. 389.

39. George A. Phoebus, *Beams of Light on Early Methodism in America* (New York: Phillips and Hunt, 1887), 27. The entry is for May 15, 16, 1785.

40. James Meacham, Journals, II, May 10, 1789 and VI, Aug. 21, 1792, in James Meacham Papers, 1788–1797, Manuscript Department, Duke University Library, Durham, N.C. Used with permission. Spelling and punctuation of original are retained. For Meacham's efforts to convince a slaveholder to manumit, see III, Apr. 17, 1790, Apr. 30, 1790, May 16, 1790, May 26, 1790, May 29, 1790 and IV, July 3, 1790. He expressed concern about slavery and slaves throughout the journals.

41. For legislative history see Mathews, *Slavery and Methodism*, and H. Shelton Smith, *In His Image, But . . .* See also William B. Gravely, "A Preacher's Covenant Against Slavery, 1795," *South Carolina United Methodist Advocate* (Columbia), March 18, 1971: 8–9, 14. Phoebus, *Beams of Light*, 137, Aug. 27, 28, 1791. Frederick E. Maser and Howard T. Maag, eds., *Journal of Joseph Pilmore, Methodist Itinerant* (Philadelphia: Message Publishing Co. for the Historical Society of the Philadelphia Annual Conference, 1969), 74, Jan. 27, 1771; 149, Aug. 9, 1772; 150, Aug. 16, 1772.

42. William Warren Sweet, *Religion on the American Frontier*, 4, 174–75.

43. Robert Paine, *Life and Times of William McKendree*, 2 vols. (Nashville: Publishing House of the Methodist Episcopal Church, South, 1874), I, 127, Oct. 30, 1790.

44. Raboteau, *Slave Religion*.

45. Mathews, *Religion in the Old South*, 185.

46. *Discipline*, 1785 p. 3. Q. 4; 1790, p. iii.

47. See chapter 3.

48. John B. Boles, *The Great Revival, 1787–1805: The Origins of the Southern Evangelical Mind* (Lexington: University Press of Kentucky, 1972). Charles A. Johnson, *The Frontier Camp Meeting: Religion's Harvest Time* (Dallas: Southern Methodist University Press, 1955). Boles and Johnson perceive the connection that we are making but construe as antecedents what is here treated as essence. However one assesses the relation, the vital point is the southern elaboration of what would become a national institution. Boles affirms: "[T]he theology and techniques of the Kentucky Revival were developed, and the personnel trained in the East "(p. x). And after Kentucky caught fire, the blaze "swept back over the entire

South with amazing rapidity, even seeping into the contiguous portions of the Ohio territory, western Pennsylvania, and Maryland. By almost instantaneously overrunning the South, the Great Revival proved itself to be more than a mere frontier aberration" (p. 70).

49. *American Methodist Pioneer, The Life and Journals of Freeborn Garrett-son,* ed. Robert D. Simpson, recently published and available through the Drew University Library, but used in manuscript. See Aug. 19, 20, 1780, and similar entries throughout.

50. R. Garrettson, "An Account of the Work of God at Petersburg, Virginia," *Arminian Magazine,* XIII (1790), 300–307, pp. 304–305. Virtually any journal from this region and this period offers similar accounts. One convenient printed source is the Ezekiel Cooper journals, excerpted by Phoebus in *Beams of Light.*

51. Isaac, *The Transformation of Virginia.* John R. Stilgoe, *Common Land-scape of America, 1580 to 1845* (New Haven: Yale University Press, 1982).

52. For further development of this argument, see chapter 2.

53. *The Doctrines and Discipline of the Methodist Episcopal Church, South,* 1846, vii, 9–12. I wish to express appreciation to my former colleagues in the Drew University Library and on the staff of the General Commission on Archives and History of the United Methodist Church for their always cordial assistance and for the use of the collections, and to Elmer and Betty O'Brien who shared insights from their indexing of the *Quarterly Reviews* which guided my research.

5. Conference as a Means of Grace

As the discussion will eventually show, the title of this chapter derives from the Methodist *Discipline* and the document from which the *Discipline* derives, Wesley's *Large Minutes.* In both, five means of grace were identified—prayer, searching the Scriptures, the Lord's Supper, fasting and Christian conference. This chapter explores conference as a means of grace, an explicitly theological formulation, for the light it sheds on the organizational structure of Methodism. It should become clear to the reader that early Methodists did not themselves attach this theological formulation to their organizational structures but that the conference structures functioned in ways and to ends that Methodists would have pronounced 'gracious'.

1. Jesse Lee, *A Short History of the Methodists* (Baltimore, 1810; facsimile ed., Rutland, Vt.: Academy Books, 1974), "Contents." These chapter titles follow an initial chapter, "Of the rise of the Methodists in England in 1729, and of the beginning of Methodism in the United States of America in 1766."

2. Ibid., 50.

3. Ibid., 52.

4. See again this first significant estimate, *A Short History of the Methodists* by Jesse Lee and the later important multivolume effort by Nathan Bangs, *A History of the Methodist Episcopal Church,* 4 vols., 12th ed. (New York: Carlton & Porter, 1860). Bangs enunciated this principle of historical analysis in a recapitulative statement bringing the reader from the beginnings of his account up to 1812 (II, 303–305).

5. Illustrations of this structure to Methodist reflections abound. One example, readily accessible, is Rev. J. B. Wakeley, ed., *The Patriarch of One Hundred Years: Being Reminiscences, Historical and Biographical of Rev. Henry Boehm,* (New York: Nelson & Phillips, 1875; repr. Lancaster, Pa.: Abram W. Sangrey, 1982). This structure shapes the chapters that treat Boehm's own active service,

chapter IV and following. Chapter IV recounts Boehm's impressions of the General Conference of 1800 and V his perceptions of the Philadelphia Conference of that year. Thereafter the chapters and narrative track Boehm's appointments, which, of course, extend from conference to conference.

6. Illustrative of how embedded in Methodist thought patterns this structure is and how readily it serves to organize Methodist experience is one of the very earliest publications of American Methodism, *The Experiences and Travels of Mr. Freeborn Garrettson, Minister of The Methodist Episcopal Church in North America* (Philadelphia: Parry Hall, 1791; reprinted in *American Methodist Pioneer: The Life and Journals of The Rev. Freeborn Garrettson, 1752–1827*, ed. Robert Drew Simpson [Rutland, Vt.: Academy Books, 1984], 35–144. This edited version is particularly valuable since it includes extensive samplings of the manuscript journals from which Garrettson assembled his volume, allowing the reader to see both the daily perceptions and Garrettson's reworking of these.) It is unfortunate that Francis Asbury's editors have imposed a modern chronology and state-by-state location on his journals rather than permitting his periodization to give them shape. See *The Journal and Letters of Francis Asbury*, 3 vols., ed. Elmer T. Clark (London: Epworth Press; Nashville: Abingdon Press, 1958), hereinafter JLFA. Compare that version with earlier ones, as for instance *Journal of Rev. Francis Asbury*, 3 vols. (New York: Eaton & Mains, 1821).

7. The best analysis of conference, W. L. Doughty's *John Wesley: His Conferences and His Preachers* (London: City Road, 1944), treats the phenomenon only in its British context. Much of what he affirms applies also to the American version.

8. On the evolution and nature of American Methodist structure see Frederick A. Norwood, "The Church Takes Shape," *The History of American Methodism*, ed. Emory S. Bucke, 3 vols. (New York & Nashville: Abingdon Press, 1964), I, 419–87. On the General Conference, see especially pp. 433 ff. Hereinafter referred to as HAM.

9. It must be conceded that some of these points do not apply uniquely to Methodism but characterize denominations generally. With respect to that, several observations should be made. First, historians should not assume that only that which distinguishes is what characterizes and confine their treatment to unique aspects of denominational life. Here we will attempt to draw out the implications of conference but recognize that some of the points, this one in particular, may apply equally to other denominations as well and may characterize their existence as well. Some things that are not distinguishing are nevertheless characterizing and deserving of careful historical treatment. Second, we will attempt to show nuances to the Methodist use of conference that may well not be shared across the range of denominations. Third, we will endeavor to bring to somewhat fuller consciousness implicit Methodist understandings of conference in the belief that Methodists would profit from sharing the ecclesial self-understanding and self-consciousness possessed by other traditions, most notably the Reformed or Calvinist tradition.

10. This is a point developed in chapter 4. That argument derives from the case made for the temporal character of Southern and Chesapeake social order, and made elegantly I would add, by Rhys Isaac in *The Transformation of Virginia, 1740–1790* (Chapel Hill: University of North Carolina Press, 1982) and by Donald G. Mathews in *Religion in the Old South* (Chicago: University of Chicago Press, 1977).

11. Lee, *Short History of the Methodists*, 234. Lee indicated that "[T]he bounds of each conference was fixed. . . . Before this regulation was established, the bishop had the power of appointing the number of conferences at his own discre-

tion" (see HAM, I, 456). The geographical meaning of conference increased as the church moved in successive General Conferences to give the annual conference boundaries. James E. Armstrong noted that as of 1802: "The term Conference now takes on a double meaning, designating, not only, as heretofore, the body of the preachers in their assemblies, but also the territory to which they are assigned," *History of the Old Baltimore Conference* (Baltimore: Printed for the Author, 1907), 131.

12. Ibid., 234.

13. Wallace Guy Smeltzer observes: "Though the geographical boundaries of the Conferences were set in 1796, it is not until after the General Conference of 1804 that the membership of the Preachers came to be considered as belonging to specific Conferences," *Methodism on the Headwaters of the Ohio: The History of the Pittsburgh Conference of the Methodist Church* (Nashville: Parthenon Press, 1951), 73.

14. "The Letters Written to Daniel Hitt, Methodist Preacher, 1788 to 1806," given to Ohio Wesleyan University. Transcript consulted at Drew University Library. E. Scholfield to Hitt, 1/28/1790, p. 26.

15. JLFA, I, 538, for early May 1787.

16. Boehm, *Reminiscences*, 180, 228. For both years Boehm traveled with Asbury and rendered his own estimate of the fraternal temperature of these affairs (195).

17. *Sketches of the Life and Travels of Rev. Thomas Ware, . . . Written by Himself* (New York, 1842; facsimile reprint by Holston Conference, 1984), 241.

18. The social cohesion can be illustrated by the accounts preachers gave of the intensity of their engagement with one another at conference. It is also illustrated by retrospective accounts of conference life. See, for instance, Pennell Coombe, *A Fifty Years' Review of the Philadelphia Annual Conference of The Methodist Episcopal Church.* Delivered before the Philadelphia Preachers' Meeting, June 18, 1883, and published by request. Also *Crowned Victors: The Memoirs of over Four Hundred Methodist Preachers,* compiled by J. W. Hedges (Baltimore: Methodist Episcopal Book Depository, 1878), which covers the church as a whole through 1829 and thereafter only the Baltimore Conference.

For other dimensions of the fraternal character of conference and of Methodism, see prior chapters.

19. That usage is magisterially expressed in the several constitutional histories of Methodism, James M. Buckley, *Constitutional and Parliamentary History of the Methodist Episcopal Church* (New York: Methodist Book Concern, 1912); Thomas B. Neely, *A History of the Origin and Development of the Governing Conference in Methodism* (Cincinnati: Curts & Jennings, 1892); Jno. J. Tigert, *A Constitutional History of American Episcopal Methodism,* 3d ed. (Nashville: Publishing House of the Methodist Episcopal Church, South, 1908); and Nolan B. Harmon, *The Organization of the Methodist Church* (New York: Abingdon-Cokesbury Press, 1948; 2nd ed., Nashville: The Methodist Publishing House, 1962).

20. In part because everything, in a sense, belonged to conference, early Methodists built on conference, employing it as foundation for other structure, tying missionary, education, publication, financial efforts to that basis. Conference, at least in its early years, gathered in the entire Methodist system.

21. The references to 'conference' in standard Methodist bibliographies, subject indices, and reference works are quite modest. For instance, *The United Methodist Periodical Index* does not employ 'conference' as an entry (note volumes for 1961–65, for 1966–70, for 1970–75 and for 1975–80). *Methodist History Index,* Volumes I–XX (Oct. 1962–July 1982) does contain four references to 'conference'

but only one of them deals explicitly and directly with the conference. *The Ency-clopedia of World Methodism,* edited by Nolan B. Harmon et al., 2 vols. (Nashville: United Methodist Publishing House, 1974), I, 558–61 offers several short articles with 'conference' in the title. Only one of the essays, "Conference, British Methodist," really focuses on the conference as a Methodist phenomenon. The *Methodist Union Catalog: Pre–1976 Imprints* edited by Kenneth E. Rowe (Metuchen, N.J. and London: Scarecrow Press, 1975-), III, does not index by subject and so gathers under 'conference' only items with that as the initial word in the title. Even so, one might expect a considerable array of books devoted to this central feature of Methodist polity. Instead, 'conference' is used primarily either in adjectival fashion (i.e., *Conference Legislation*) or independently of its Methodist meaning (i.e. *Conference on Human Relations*). Rowe's exhaustive inventory tells the story. Methodists have been strangely uninterested in interpreting their most basic ecclesial feature.

This is not to say that we want for books having to do with the conference. Methodist libraries teem with conference histories. However, these treat specific conference sagas. Seldom do they step back to analyze the conference as a phenomenon. The main resources remain Neely, *The Governing Conference in Methodism*; Tigert, *Constitutional History of American Episcopal Methodism,* and Buckley, *Constitutional and Parliamentary History of the Methodist Episcopal Church.*

One looks in vain for intellectual or theological assessments. Conference belongs to the category of polity and that alone. That is graphically illustrated in the *Index to the Methodist Quarterly Review . . . 1818–1881* by Elijah H. Pilcher (New York: Phillips & Hunt, 1884), perhaps the best indication of nineteenth century Methodism's reflection on itself. It arrays topics under a variety of headings: theological, ecclesiastical, etc. Conference belongs clearly to the latter and that only.

22. *American Methodist Pioneer,* 173. Simpson injects a note into this last entry identifying Megan and Neal as two clergy members of the Church of England, Samuel Magaw and Hugh Neill, who sympathized with and supported the Methodists.

23. It is the point of this and the prior chapter that Methodism's sense of what constituted 'church' was richer and more nuanced than this formal and explicit statement thereof. Here we want only to establish that by its own formal and theological definition—that in the Articles of Religion, the classic Reformation definition, the one borrowed from Anglicanism—Methodism came most fully to ecclesial status in the quarterly meeting.

24. Article XIII—Of the Church. The Articles are, of course, those of the Church of England, as adapted for the American Methodists by Wesley (and in the case of one article perhaps Thomas Coke or the Christmas Conference). See Tigert, *A Constitutional History of American Episcopal Methodism,* 465.

25. George A. Phoebus, *Beams of Light on Early Methodism in America* (New York: Phillips and Hunt, 1887), 80–81.

26. Lee, *Short History,* 55–56, 130–33, 275, 285, 138–40, 145–46, 271–75. Not all the revivals were connected with conferences. See those reported on pp. 43, 49, 77, 89, 216, and 277.

27. Leland Scott in "The Message of Early American Methodism," HAM, I, 308, observes, "The message of early American Methodism cannot be separated from its media."

28. These points are made in different form by Doughty, *John Wesley: His Conferences.* Doughty indicated: "the Conference steadily grew in influence and popularity and speedily became the focal point of Methodist religious life. . . . Its

meeting places were London, Bristol, and Leeds, and the Methodists in those areas eagerly anticipated its coming and shared joyously in its many public ministrations. Round it gathered the loving, reverent thoughts and for it rose the prayers of the Methodist people everywhere. It became the symbol of their unity; the grand climax of their year; an incentive to more intense missionary enterprise and the fount of inspiration for a deeper personal consecration" (27).

29. John Lawson, "The People called Methodists—2. 'Our Discipline,' " *A History of the Methodist Church in Great Britain,* ed. Rupert Davies and Gordon Rupp (London: Epworth Press, 1965), I, 185.

30. See Tigert, *A Constitutional History of American Episcopal Methodism,* 575–76. This section of Tigert's work parallels "The Large Minutes" with the first *Discipline* of the American church. The five means of grace were taken over intact into the *Discipline.*

The five were prayer, searching the Scriptures, the Lord's Supper, fasting, and Christian conference. These he termed "Instituted" means of grace. He also recognized "Prudential" means of grace, a series of guidelines for Christian existence, largely Pietist in their origin, which he particularized for all Christians, for preachers, and for his assistants.

31. Ibid., 576.

32. Conference was the way Wesley sought to conduct his affairs with his people. Although Mr. Wesley would find those of the late twentieth century very strange affairs, they bear the marks and carry on the functions that he, and perhaps even his mother, intended as Christian conference. Indeed, conferences recalled the patterns of engagement of the Wesley home and even to this day they remain something of a family affair.

33. The titles of the several editions of these varied.

34. "John Bennet's Copy of the Minutes of the Conferences of 1744, 1745, 1747 and 1748; With Wesley's Copy of Those for 1745." *Publications of The Wesley Historical Society,* I (1896), 39.

35. Ibid., 49–50. In the Large Minutes this question was recast: "Do we sufficiently watch over our Helpers?" *The first American Discipline reshaped that into "Do we sufficiently watch over each other?"* The Large Minutes continued with the sentence about helper as pupil. The American Discipline omitted that. Both then continued with a recast version of the counsel; the British version continued the Wesleyan oversight; the American persisted in rendering Wesley's paternal venture in fraternal language:

> Should we not frequently ask each other, Do you walk closely with God? Have you *now* Fellowship with the Father and the Son? At what Hour do you rise? Do you punctually observe the Morning and Evening Hour of Retirement? Do you spend the Day in the Manner which the Conference advises? [British version 'which we advise?'] Do you converse seriously, usefully and closely? (Tigert, *A Constitutional History of American Episcopal Methodism,* 575).

In the Large Minutes this question was expanded to include also the query about use of the Means of Grace: "Do you use all the Means of Grace yourself, and inforce the use of them on all other persons?" Then followed the distinction, "They are either *Instituted* or *Prudential,*" and also the enumeration detailed in a prior note. See Tigert, 575–76.

36. Ibid., 53. "Q. What further advice can be given to our Assistants in order to their confiding in each other? A. Let them beware how they despise each other's gifts, and much more how they speak anything bordering thereon. 2. Let them

never speak slightly of each other in any kind. 3. Let them defend one another's character in every point to the uttermost of their power. 4. Let them labour in honor each to prefer the other to himself" (54). In the Large Minutes and the First Discipline of the MEC (Q. 67 of the latter), the above and those cited in the text were worked into an eight-point answer. See Tigert, *A Constitutional History of American Episcopal Methodism*, 578.

37. To have done so might well have compromised Methodism's relation with The Church of England. To draw the theological implications of conference would be to think about it ecclesiologically. That Wesley could not afford to do. He could not continue to hold the movement within the Church, to insist that Methodists really sustain their participation, to make good on his claim to be a reforming effort from within—if he talked and wrote about the gracious and ecclesial dimensions of conference.

38. Early Methodists did not employ the term "orthopraxy' for this pragmatism but the notion is now used to suggest what early Methodists would have indeed affirmed, namely that they adopted means because they worked "to the glory of God." There was, then, a proportionality between means and ends. Some things that might—indeed did—produce results were deemed unacceptable.

39. They too were so by definition (if only implicitly), by design and procedure, by expectation, by the rules and regimen through which they operated, by the way they conducted business, by their clear sense of the redemptive activities which should be carried out for the surrounding community and local Methodists, by the intense scrutiny and discipline exercised over members, by the intimacy developed and by the unity achieved. The discussion turns now to exploration of these features of conference.

40. See Tigert, *Constitutional History*, 575–76.

41. "Journals," II for Feb. 10, 1789, and throughout III in James Meacham Papers, 1788–1797, Manuscript Department, Duke University Library; used with permission. Garrettson described the 1784 (May) conference as "a sweet meeting," and quarterly meetings as a "sweet time." *American Religious Pioneer*, 240, 241 for May 26 and July 25, 1784.

42. *Experience and Travels*, Section IV, 67; in *American Methodist Pioneer*, 62. Thomas Coke observed the fruits of the Spirit in a 1796 Virginia Conference, "Nothing but love, peace, joy, unity and concord, I may truly say, manifested themselves in this Conference." *Extracts of the Journals of . . . Thomas Coke* (Dublin, 1816), 235.

43. *The Patriarch of One Hundred Years*, 180. See also his description of the spiritual quality of the General Conference of 1808, 180–84.

44. William W. Bennett, *Memorials of Methodism in Virginia*, 2d. ed. (Richmond: Published by the Author, 1871), pp. 306–308. Compare the detailed account given by James Meacham of the 1794 Petersburg Conference and the prominence therein of the relation of experiences and attention to the spiritual development of the preachers (James Meacham Papers, 1788–1797).

45. Coke, *Extracts of the Journals of . . . Thomas Coke*, 174. Of this 1791 conference in North Carolina, Coke had already observed:

> At this Conference, a remarkable spirit of prayer was poured forth on the Preachers. Every night, before we concluded, Heaven itself seemed to be opened to our believing souls. One of the Preachers was so blessed in the course of our prayers that he was constrained to cry, "O I never was so happy in all my life before! O what a heaven of heavens I feel."

Compare remarks on other conferences that year, pp. 171, 175. Note also his comment on the Virginia conference of 1796:

> After the necessary business was finished, we spent about two days in band, each preacher in his turn relating the experiences of his own soul, and the success of his ministry for the last year. It was a profit-able season. I wish this useful method was pursued, as far as possible, in our European Conferences. (235)

This last observation and Coke's comment on the novelty of American proceed-ings deserve special attention. The 'gracious' or revivalistic character of American conferences may or may not have differed from or exceeded that of the parent body. It was nevertheless an aspect of the American movement that Coke recog-nized as important. That is the important recognition.

46. These are published as *The Rise of Methodism in the West: Being the Jour-nal of the Western Conference, 1800–1811*, ed. William Warren Sweet (New York & Cincinnati: Methodist Book Concern; Nashville, Dallas, Richmond: Smith & La-mar, 1920). Minutes for this particular conference session constitute pages 100–109.

47. Ibid., 101.

48. Ibid., 101–109.

49. Ibid., 101.

50. Ibid., 101–102.

51. Ibid., 107.

52. Ibid., 107 (the *Journal* did not indicate but Asbury did that he preached the Sunday of conference week "to about three thousand souls," Sweet's note, p. 108).

53. As I have observed in a previous note, "The Letters Written to Daniel Hitt" are a remarkable index of the covenantal bonds between and among the Methodist preachers. Robert Manley wrote to Hitt in this fashion:

> Brother when I say that I love you, GOD bears witness to the truth of what I say: I have not forgot the hours, days, weeks, months & may I not say years, that we have spent together; how many fatigueing rides over the hills, thro mud & water, thro heat & cold in order to discharge our duty to GOD, ourselves & fellowmen, how many meetings have we attended together? how often have I heard your voice, praying for, & crying to sinners to turn to GOD, to mourners to believe in Jesus, and to believers to be faithful till death? I have to stop, to wipe the silent tear that runs down my cheeks. O! shall we meet in happiness no more to part? I hope we shall. Pray for me, I trust to do the same for you. The family are all well in body. & I trust striving for heaven & happi-ness. . . . (Typescript, 265–66, 9/13/1801)

54. Bennett, *Memorials of Methodism in Virginia*, 195.

55. The 1800 General Conference was the scene of a well-attested revival, "the greatest that has ever occurred during the session of any General Conference," according to Boehm, *The Patriarch of One Hundred Years*, 35–43. Boehm pro-vided insightful portrayals of revivalistic endeavor at that conference. As a visitor, Boehm spent time at and described the preaching, protracted prayer–meetings and street singing that produced hundreds of conversions. He gave comparably detailed descriptions of revivals at annual and quarterly meetings as well.

56. This argument is more fully developed and the evidence examined in chapter 2.

6. The Four Languages of Early American Methodism

1. Minton Thrift, *Memoir of the Rev. Jesse Lee. With Extracts from His Journals* (New York: N. Bangs and T. Mason for the Methodist Episcopal Church, 1823), 208–209. As the first great American-born leader of the movement, Lee gave voice to American Methodism. Note particularly the language: melting, weeping, singing, trembling, crying, revive. This strongly biblical and vernacular rhetoric typifies Methodist journals. It is a biblical vernacular, a biblical pietist vernacular, a biblical Wesleyan vernacular.

2. Jesse Lee gave some indication of his understanding of and commitment to this loud Methodist voice in Fairfield, August 13th [1789]: "After meeting was over, a man came to me and said the women complained that I preached so loud that it made their heads ache, and they wished me to speak a little lower the next time I came: but I hope God will help me to speak hereafter, so as to make their hearts ache." Ibid., 120.

3. Lee, of course, took Methodism into the Calvinist stronghold of New England. An entry of 1795 typifies his stance: "At night, I preached at doctor Hind's, on Rom. ix. 22. Here I endeavoured to show the unreasonableness of predestination; and how the people had fitted themselves for destruction; and yet, God had much long-suffering towards them. I further told them, a minister ought to pray the people, in Christ's stead, to be reconciled to God, warn them of their danger, and weep over them, and let them know that the Lord was not willing that they should be damned; but that they should come to the knowledge of the truth and be saved. I also endeavoured to show how unreasonable it was for a minister to say that God was willing to send his hearers to hell; and that they should bless God for sending them there. I had a comfortable meeting, and freedom in speaking. Just as I was going to leave the house, the minister came in, and abundance of people flocked into the room, expecting to hear us dispute, but after asking him a few questions *civilly*, we parted." Ibid., 215–16.

4. The finding of the voice was often traumatic. Lee reported the following concerning his first effort at preaching: "On the 17th of November, 1779, I preached for the first time in my life, at a place called the Old Barn." He preached several times soon thereafter, "and found much of the Divine Presence with me in public, yet I was so sensible of my own weakness and insufficiency, that after I had preached, I would retire to the woods and prostrate myself on the ground, and weep before the Lord, and pray that he would pardon the imperfections of my preaching, and give me strength to declare his whole counsel in purity. . . . " Ibid., 22.

5. Harry S. Stout in *The New England Soul: Preaching and Religious Culture in Colonial New England* (New York: Oxford University Press, 1986) argues that the Great Awakening wrought a revolution in American discourse and this rhetorical revolution made possible the political revolution.

6. The people responded in kind. They also shouted, or, as in this case with Lee in 1799, they roared: "Sunday, 10th [February 1799]. At Charlotte meeting-house, Mr. Asbury preached, and after an intermission of fifteen minutes, I preached. God was in the midst of us. Several young converts were present; and they, with others, were deeply melted into tears; some of them could hardly refrain from roaring

aloud. Glory be to God in the highest, for this meeting." *Memoir of the Rev. Jesse Lee,* 144, 247.

7. The term 'language' in this paper obviously overstates the separateness and incompatibility of what might more judiciously be described as paradigm, frame of reference, meaning system. However, 'language' does underscore problems of translation, mutual intelligibility, multiple reference, divergent meanings which this paper argues did haunt Methodist terminology. The use here is heuristic.

8. In *The Garden of American Methodism: The Delmarva Peninsula, 1769–1820* (Wilmington, Del.: Scholarly Resources, 1984), William H. Williams suggests that Methodism's viability as a second English church was one source of its attractiveness (89–120).

9. The literature on republicanism is immense. See the helpful discussions thereof by Robert E. Shalhope, "Republicanism and Early American Historiography," *William and Mary Quarterly,* 3d ser. 39 (Apr. 1982), 334–56, and "Toward a Republican Synthesis: The Emergence of an Understanding of Republicanism in American Historiography," *William and Mary Quarterly,* 3d ser. 29 (Jan. 1972), 49–80. See also Isaac Kramnick, "Republican Revisionism Revisited," *American Historical Review,* 87 (June 1982), 629–64.

10. One could certainly illustrate these four languages with texts from most years after 1800. The choice of 1798 is somewhat arbitrary. As we shall see, it does afford us one of the earliest clear expressions of Methodism's adoption of republican ideas and a very powerful illustration of Methodism's episcopal self-understanding. Popular and Wesleyan language abound at all times. One virtue of such an early year is that we can see these several voices of Methodism in relative 'pure' form. For these reasons, the choice of 1798 seemed apt.

11. *Memoir of the Rev. Jesse Lee,* 236.

12. Ibid., 202, 203, 204, 205. Lee traveled then in New England.

13. For the roles of Dickins and Cooper in the Methodist book enterprise and the publications overwhich they exercised oversight, consult James Penn Pilkington, *The Methodist Publishing House. A History,* 2 vols. (Nashville: Abingdon Press, 1968; 1988), I, 63–148.

14. Eventually, American Methodist serials would lend themselves to the popular idiom. *The Methodist Magazine, for the Year 1798* (Philadelphia, 1798) carried a subtitle that suggested such a purpose: "Containing Original Sermons, Experiences, Letters, and Other Religious Pieces; Together with Instructive and Useful Extracts from Different Authors." This was American Methodism's second effort at a serious magazine and the second (and final) year of the experiment. It could have passed as a British publication, for it carried virtually nothing American and was heavily dominated by Wesley's sermons, writings and collected material. As such, it transmitted the Wesleyan idiom.

15. *The Doctrines and Discipline of the Methodist Episcopal Church in America, with Explanatory Notes, by Thomas Coke and Francis Asbury* (Philadelphia, 1798); facsimile edition, edited by Frederick A. Norwood (Rutland, Vt.: Academy Books, 1979), 70. The 1796 General Conference had authorized the publication of *The Methodist Magazine* with this notation: "N.B. The propagation of religious knowledge by the means of the press, is next in importance to the preaching of the gospel. To supply the people therefore with the most pious and useful books, in order that they may fill up their leisure hours in the most profitable ways, is an object worthy the deepest attention of their pastors." *Minutes of the General Conference of the Methodist Episcopal Church . . . 1796* (Baltimore, 1796), 15.

16. *Doctrines and Discipline,* iv., Advertisement to the Reader: "The last General Conference desired the Bishops to draw up Annotations on the Form of the

Discipline. . . . " In his "Introduction," Norwood argues that O'Kelly's movement motivated these annotations.

17. Ibid., 6. The italics appeared in the original.

18. Neither, however, made clear reference to the actual service to be used. Ibid., 118–20.

19. On the character of colonial Anglicanism see Frederick V. Mills, Sr., *Bishops by Ballot* (New York: Oxford University Press, 1978), and Henry F. May, *The Enlightenment in America* (New York: Oxford University Press, 1976).

20. *Doctrines and Discipline of the Methodist Episcopal Church in America, with Explanatory Notes,* 40.

21. On O'Kelly and these events, see *The History of American Methodism,* ed. Emory S. Bucke, 3 vols. (New York: Abingdon Press, 1964), I, pp; 429–52.

22. William Warren Sweet acknowledged losses to the Methodist Episcopal Church in 1795–96 of almost 10,000 but attributed some of that to other causes. *Methodism in American History,* rev. ed. (New York: Abingdon Press, 1953), 134.

23. James O'Kelly, *The Author's Apology for Protesting Against the Methodist Episcopal Government* (Richmond: John Dixon, 1798).

24. Ibid., 4, 9, 21, 38.

25. For historiographical treatment of this tradition, see note 8 above. Classic treatment can be found in Caroline Robbins, *The Eighteenth-Century Commonwealthman* (Cambridge, Mass.: Harvard University Press, 1959), Bernard Bailyn, *The Ideological Origins of the American Revolution* (Cambridge, Mass.: Harvard University Press, 1967), and Gordon S. Wood, *The Creation of the American Republic* (New York: W. W. Norton & Company, 1972).

26. On the prevalence of conspiratorial visions and the underlying causes thereof, see the brilliant exposition by Gordon S. Wood, "Conspiracy and the Paranoid Style: Causality and Deceit in the Eighteenth Century," *William and Mary Quarterly,* 3d ser. 39 (July 1982), 401–41.

27. Nathan O. Hatch examines this preaching and the longer political experience that gave shape to it in *The Sacred Cause of Liberty* (New Haven: Yale University Press, 1977), 139–75.

28. These developments are treated in a variety of works. See especially Fred J. Hood, *Reformed America* (University: University of Alabama Press, 1980); Robert T. Handy, *A Christian America,* 2d ed. (New York: Oxford University Press, 1984); John F. Wilson, *Public Religion in American Culture* (Philadelphia: Temple University Press, 1979); and Martin E. Marty, *Religion and Republic* (Boston: Beacon Press, 1987).

29. This point is worked out in greater detail in my forthcoming essay, "History as a Bearer of Denominational Identity: Methodism as a Case Study." ·

30. *Minutes of the Methodist Conferences, Annually Held in America; From 1773 to 1813, Inclusive* (New York: Published by Daniel Hitt and Thomas Ware, for the Methodist Connexion in the United States, 1813). "Minutes Taken at the Several Annual Conferences of the Methodist Episcopal Church, for the year 1798," 200–15.

31. Ibid., 201–204.

32. There is some question as to whether Methodism ever fully integrated those two though it brought them into sufficient coherence for the polity to work.

33. Ibid., 205. The line from Dickins appeared in italics in the original.

34. *Memoir of the Rev. Jesse Lee,* 230–40.

35. Conception here refers to both the coming to understanding and the coming into being. For discussion of the variety of tensions in Methodist understanding of ministry, see my colleague Dennis M. Campbell's excellent volume, *The Yoke of*

Obedience: The Meaning of Ordination in Methodism (Nashville: Abingdon Press, 1988), especially 72–97.

36. The literary fare for the Methodist faithful constituted an impressive and meaty diet. In the year 1798, for instance, Dickins placed this advertisement in the rear of the *Pocket Hymn Book:*

> The Following Books are Published by John Dickins . . . For the Use of the Methodist Societies in the United States of America . . . Sold by the Publisher, and the Ministers and Preachers in the several Circuits.
> The Arminian Magazine
> Thomas a Kempis
> The Form of Discipline . . . with Treatises on Predestination, Perseverance, Christian Perfection, &c.
> The Form of Discipline . . . with Explanatory Notes
> The Experience and Travel of Mr. Freeborn Garrettson
> An Extract on Infant Baptism
> Children's Instructions
> An Abridgement of Mrs. Rowe's Devout Exercises of the Heart
> The excellent Works of the Rev. Mr. John Fletcher, complete, in six volumes
> A Funeral Discourse on the Death of . . . John Wesley
> The Saints' Everlasting Rest
> The 1st volume of Mr. Francis Asbury's Journal
> A Tract on Slavery
> The Rev. John Wesley's Journal, vol. 1st.
> The Family Adviser and primitive Physic
> The Rev. John Wesley's Life
> Spiritual Letters, &c. by the Rev. John Fletcher
> Sermons by the Rev. John Wesley . . . 1st and 2nd vols.
> Doddridge's Sermons to Young People
> A Scriptural Catechism
> Minutes of the Methodist Conferences . . . 1773 to 1794 inclusive
> The same, for several late years, separately
> The Life of Monsieur De Renty
> Jane Cooper's Life and Letters
> Nicodemus, a Treatise on the Fear of Man
> Defense of Methodism
> Manners of the Ancient Christians
> Dr. Coke's Four Sermons
> The Methodist Magazine

37. Thomas Coke, *The Substance of a Sermon, Preached at Baltimore . . . Before the General Conference of the Methodist Episcopal Church, on the 27th of December, 1784, at the Ordination of the Rev. Francis Asbury to the Office of a Superintendent* (London, 1785).

38. *The Journal and Letters of Francis Asbury,* ed. Elmer T. Clark et al., 3 vols. (London: Epworth Press; Nashville: Abingdon Press, 1958), III, 475–92 (hereafter JLFA). This statement was an oral publication.

39. For the controversies that elicited these defenses, see "Anti-Methodist Publications (American)" by my Duke colleague Lawrence O. Kline, *The Encyclopedia of World Methodism,* ed. Nolan B. Harmon, 2 vols. (Nashville: United Methodist Publishing House, 1974), I, 115–19.

40. *Minutes of the Methodist Conferences, Annually Held in America; From 1773 to 1813, Inclusive*, 162–64.

41. These were the questions Wesley posed at the first conference, questions that, over time, generated the structure and emphases of the Methodist *Large Minutes* and *Discipline*. "Minutes of Some Late Conversations Between the Rev. Mr. Wesley and Others," *The Works of John Wesley*, Jackson edition, 14 vols. (London, 1872: Grand Rapids: Zondervan, 1958), VIII, 275.

42. *Doctrines and Discipline of the Methodist Episcopal Church in America, with Explanatory Notes*, 18.

43. JLFA II, 46. The entry is March 30, 1795.

44. This point is rather fully treated in chapter 5.

45. This point is elaborated in chapter 3.

46. That phrase, from G. K. Chesterton, forms the title and motif of Sidney E. Mead's book (New York: Harper & Row, Publishers, 1975).

47. The other points in this litany have been, at least, hinted at. Although the subject deserves more attention than can be given here, we should note that the several languages did conceive and invoke authority in distinctive fashion. That can be illustrated by reference to what has recently been regarded as a distinctively Wesleyan or Methodist (also distinctively Anglican and Catholic) conception of authority. Wesley and Methodists purportedly appeal to a four-fold scheme of authority, the so-called Wesleyan quadrilateral—scripture, tradition, reason and experience. On one cut through these languages, we might associate the elements of the quadrilateral respectively with popular, episcopal, republican and Wesleyan languages. There is, in fact, some correspondence here: popular (scripture), episcopal (tradition), republican (reason), and Wesleyan (experience).

At a deeper level of analysis, we would need to recognize each of the languages as possessing its own notion of the four elements that constitute the quadrilateral. For instance, the republican language had its own hermeneutic for reading scripture, a very covenantal one, much commented upon in historical and literary studies of Puritanism (see, for instance, the work of Sacvan Bercovitch). The republican sense of tradition, of history as the struggle between liberty and tyranny, and of golden ages of republican government, we have already noted. For republicanism, reason seemed, at times, a virtual idol. To be sure, what Republicans meant by 'reason' changed. Reason had strongly empirical, Lockean overtones until those were recast by the Scottish Common Sense philsophers. Common sense became powerful among Methodists as among other Protestants. At that point, the line between reason and experience grew indistinct. Republican views of experience were affected by this shift in epistemology. Increasingly in the nineteenth century, experience was construed as common sense. Appeal to American experience, to American common sense also become common.

It would be easy to show that the other languages had their conceptions of the elements of this quadrilateral. The point of this excursus is to underscore the integrity of these languages and the divergent ways in which they pulled.

Index

Abolitionism: Edenic quality of early
Methodism, xii. *See also* Slavery
African Methodist Episcopal Zion Church:
languages and ecclesiologies, 96
Alcoholics Anonymous: Methodist formula
of shared experience, 4
Allen, Richard: southern leadership of early
Methodism, 53; Black Methodist leaders,
60
America: continuity between Wesley and,
xiv–xv; Asbury's concept of, 36–37;
ambivalence of Methodist proclamations
about nation, 39–40, 110n; post-
revolutionary and public theology, 90.
See also Nation; Continent
Americanization: Methodist historiography,
xiv–xv; Asbury's concept of, 36
American Revolution: Methodism as
revolutionary movement, xv; Methodist
views of political society, 35, 37–38;
republican language, 84; O'Kelly and
ideology, 89; Garrettson's journals, 101n,
111n–112n; southern origins of
American Methodism, 115n
Anglicanism: episcopal language, xvii, 87–
88; evangelicalism as alternative to
patriarchal, 55–58. *See also* Church of
England
Apotheosis: implications of linguistic
imprecision, 16
Articles of Religion: unity of organization
and life, 19
Asbury, Francis: metaphor of glass to heart,
xvi, 33, 44, 110n; rejection of language
and values, xviii; community, fraternity,
and order in journal entries, 1–2; use of
term "melting," 3; description of love
feast, 4; traveling preachers, 8, 10; order
and conferences, 11–13; quarterly
meetings, 14, 27, 28, 107n–108n; camp
meetings, 22, 23, 31, 106n; conferences
and revivalism, 29; on temporal power,
33; concept of continent and nation, 36–
37; American Revolution, 37; political
passivity, 41; continental orientation, 41,
42; use of term "Zion," 42, 43;
movement of Methodism from south to
west, 52; fraternity and conferences, 67;

American Methodism and Church of
England, 86; episcopal language, 87–88;
O'Kelly as threat, 90; popular language
and doctrine, 95; publication of journals,
120n
Atlas of Early American History
(Cappon): southern orientation of
American Methodism, 51
Authority: Methodist concept and
languages, 130n
*The Author's Apology for Protesting
Against the Methodist Episcopal
Government* (O'Kelly): republican
language, 88–89

Baker, Frank: Methodism and Anglicanism,
56
Baltimore: history of American Methodism,
51
Bangs, Nathan: Zion and American
Methodism, 43; Methodist history and
republicanism, 91
Baptism: evangelicalism and patriarchal
Anglicanism, 56
Bible: New Testament and episcopal
language, 87, 88; popular language, 94–
95, 101n, 126n; republican language,
130n
Biformity: Methodists and American
nationality, 34
Blacks: Edenic quality of early Methodism,
xii; community in early Methodism, 5;
use of term "brother," 6; exclusion from
ministry, 18; retention of radical
messages latent in Methodist rhetoric
and lifestyle, 57–58; early Methodism as
biracial movement, 59–60; appeal of
popular Methodism, 96; early appearance
of segregation, 108n; distinctive religious
experience in South, 115n. *See also*
Racism; Slavery
Bledsoe, A. T.: conference legislation on
slavery, 58
Boehm, Henry: fraternity and conference,
67–68; revival and conference, 125n
Boehm, Martin: conferences and
spirituality, 75
Boles, John B.: camp meetings, 22

131

RUSSELL E. RICHEY is Associate Dean for Academic Programs and Research Professor of Church History at the Divinity School, Duke University. He is the editor of *Rethinking Methodist History* and a forthcoming volume on the scholarly writing of denominational history. He is also the secretary of the newly organized Historical Society of The United Methodist Church.